Planet Earth University

The Art of Living Aligned

By Jessica Meléndez

Founder of ESCANVI Services

Certified Clinical & Transpersonal Hypnotherapist

PMP® | Conscious Leadership & Emotional Healing

www.escanviservices.com

@escanviservices.jessica

ESCANVI Press

First Edition: June 2025
Published by ESCANVI Press
Orlando, FL
www.escanviservices.com

ISBN: 978-1-968313-00-5

I lovingly dedicate this book to my son—Thank you so much for choosing me as your mother. Your presence made me rise. Your strength gave me courage. Your soul continues to uplift and inspire mine. You are my greatest teacher.

To my younger self—I see you now. I believe you. I love you. You never had to earn your worth. You were always and already the light.

And to every soul who finds these pages—This is for you. For the parts of you that felt too much, too tender, too strange. For the moments you doubted your magic. For the times you almost gave up.

May this book remind you: You are not alone. You are not broken. You are becoming, unfolding, blossoming …

And your story is medicine—for you, and for the world.

CONTENTS

A Whisper Before We Begin

This is not a textbook.
It's a trail of breadcrumbs.
Scattered gently, intentionally—
Enneagram, Human Design,
Map of Consciousness, and more.

I won't pause to define them all.
That's not the purpose here.

They're just the echoes of what found me
when I was ready to be found.
The keys that unlocked doors in my healing,
the whispers that stirred something ancient in my bones.

And so I leave them here—
not as explanations, but as invitations.
Not as instructions, but as sparks.

If something calls to you—
let it.
If a word glows or lingers,
follow it.
If your inner child perks up,
eyes wide with wonder,
let them lead the way.

This book is a treasure map,
and you are the one holding the compass.

Trust what pulls you.
Leave what doesn't.

But know this:
Every breadcrumb I've dropped
was placed with love,
so that something in you might remember.

Prologue: The Seed Was Planted

This book didn't start as a book.

It started as a whisper.

A breadcrumb.

A moment that sparked something alive in me and refused to dim.

It was during a weekend workshop on the Enneagram, led by a professor who said something I still hear echoing in my cells:

"We are all born with three core lessons to learn in this lifetime. Earth is a university for the soul."

He laid them out like a sacred syllabus:

1. Learn self-love.

2. Enjoy your life.

3. Witness and fully appreciate the beauty within and around you.

That moment struck a chord in me so deep, it felt ancient.

I didn't just understand what he was saying: I *remembered* it.

My soul lit up.

Finally, someone had given language to what I had always felt but never fully articulated:

Life isn't random. It's a curriculum.

We don't just come here to survive.
We come to grow. To feel. To awaken. To embody truth.
And if we're lucky—to love the hell out of our human experience.

Another realization from that same weekend peeled back yet another layer.

I had always identified as an Enneagram 8—The Challenger, the strong one, the protector.
But something didn't quite fit.
And in that room, with all my masks laid bare in front of me, I discovered that, at my core, I really wasn't an 8.
Instead, I was a 4.

The Individualist.
The deep feeler.
The seeker of authenticity.

I had been performing as an 8 for most of my life—because that's what kept me safe. That's what helped me survive.
But I was now ready, finally, to soften into the truth of who I

really was.

And that shift changed everything.

That same professor who introduced me to the Enneagram also shared a parable I'll never forget.

He looked at me and said,

"You're like an eagle who was raised among chickens. You learned their ways, you lived their rhythms, and for a while, you forgot you were born to soar. But it's time now. It's time to remember who you are—and to fly."

His words struck something deep within me—not in judgment of where I came from, but as a recognition of how easy it is to internalize the limitations of the environments we grow up in.

There was nothing wrong with the people around me; they were doing their best, just as I was.
But I had spent years dimming my light, second-guessing my worth, and trying to fit in with what felt safe and familiar.

The truth is, I wasn't meant to blend in.
I was meant to rise!
And so are you.

We all come into this world with unique gifts.

But sometimes, we forget.

We adapt. We shrink to survive.

That parable wasn't just a metaphor for my life—it was a soul invitation.

An invitation to remember my truth.

To stop living from borrowed beliefs that never fit me in the first place.

It was never about blame.

It was always about remembrance.

Learning I was a 4 gave me something I didn't even know I was missing: permission to feel.

Permission to create.

Permission to be tender and real and expressive.

For the first time, I stopped seeing my sensitivity as weakness—and began to nurture the softer, artistic side of myself, which I had long buried beneath the need for survival.

It reminded me that my power wasn't in pretending to be strong.

It was in living as my true, open-hearted self.

That Enneagram weekend was the seed.
But it wasn't the only breadcrumb the Universe would drop.

Months earlier, during a Family Constellation session, I heard
a question that changed my life.
Someone in the room was struggling to find clarity, and the
facilitator casually asked,

"What's her Human Design?"

I had never heard of that concept before.
But something in me perked up.

Jessica, put it in your databank. Look it up later.

But what stirred something deep within me during the session
wasn't this question itself; rather, it was the subsequent
realization that, since early childhood, I had been carrying
suppressed rage.
Rage I didn't know I had, because I had never felt safe
enough to feel it.

That moment allowed me to finally name what had been
trapped in my body for decades.
I didn't have to stay silent.
I didn't have to bear it all alone.

That single realization created a ripple—a doorway I would later walk through in hypnotherapy, where deeper layers of healing would begin.

It was Fall Equinox night, September 22, 2023.
I was still in corporate.
Still performing.
Still pushing through a life that no longer fit.

But I followed the nudge.
And that's when I discovered something that would change everything:

I'm a Projector with Self-Projected Authority.

At the time, I didn't fully understand what that meant. So, I started learning.

Human Design is a spiritual and energetic system that blends astrology, the I Ching, the chakra system, and quantum physics.
It reveals your soul's blueprint—how your energy is designed to move through the world.

There are five main types in Human Design:

- Generators: the energizers, who are here to build and light up when doing what they love.

- Manifesting Generators: fast-moving multitaskers who thrive when they follow nonlinear joy.

- Manifestors: the initiators, bold and independent.

- Reflectors: the mirrors of society, deeply sensitive and tuned into collective energy.

- And then the Projectors: the guides, here not to do all the work, but to see the big picture, to offer wisdom, to direct energy rather than generate it.

When I found out I was a Projector, it all made sense.

The burnout. The emotional crashes.
The deep exhaustion after trying to keep up in a world that rewarded output over presence.

I wasn't here to hustle. I was here to see, to guide, to speak—from the deepest truth of who I am.

And my authority—*Self-Projected*—meant I was here to lead from my identity. From my truth.
Not from logic or pressure or shoulds, but from the clear voice of my soul.

The Universe had been sending breadcrumbs all along.

First, the Enneagram 4—reminding me I wasn't here to be strong, masked, and performative…

I was here to feel deeply, to express, to live as my authentic self.

Then, Human Design—showing me the energetic design of who I actually am.
That I'm not here to grind or chase.
I'm here to wait for recognition—to live in my truth, to shine authentically, and to allow the right people and opportunities to find me when they're aligned.

In Human Design, this is the strategy of the Projector: we don't force. We wait to be seen. When someone truly recognizes us—our presence, our wisdom, our frequency—that's when the magic flows.

Each breadcrumb was sacred.
Each one brought me closer to the remembering.
Closer to my essence.

That's when the shift began—not from outside pressure, but from inner permission.

I stopped asking, *"What should I do?"*
And instead began to ask, *"Who am I here to be?"*

That's when I knew: this book had to be born.
Because no one teaches us this.

No one teaches us how to live aligned.

How to honor our energy.

How to feel, how to love, how to return to ourselves.

We're all enrolled in Planet Earth University—

but no one hands us the syllabus.

This book is the syllabus I wish I had.

A reminder that your feelings matter.

Your design matters.

Your story, your softness, your sovereignty—it all matters.

This isn't just a book.

It's a remembering.

Welcome to the university.

Your soul already enrolled.

Now let's begin remembering why you came.

Introduction

Welcome to the University You Didn't Know You Enrolled In

No one hands you a syllabus when you're born. There's no orientation week. No map. No advisor to walk you through the course requirements.

But make no mistake—if you're reading this, you've already been enrolled.

Welcome to Planet Earth University.

Where the lessons come disguised as breakups, breakthroughs, burnout, illness, love, loss, betrayal, joy, grief, synchronicities, and second chances.

Where your soul signs you up for classes you didn't consciously choose—but absolutely needed.

Where your diploma isn't a title or a trophy, but the day you finally say:

"This is who I am—and I'm not abandoning myself again."

You came to Earth for a reason.

Not just to survive—but to *remember*.

This book is not a textbook.

It's a mirror.

A remembering.

A sacred syllabus written not with ink, but with soul.

You are not here to fix yourself. You are here to remember yourself.

Like the tide returning to shore—your truth was never gone, only waiting.

You are not broken. You are awakening.

Like morning light through a cracked window—subtle, but undeniable.

You are not too much. You are sacred.

You are not lost. You are returning.

I wrote this book not from a state of perfection, but from the spiral of healing. From the trenches. From the tenderness. From the mountaintops I've crawled my way toward after collapsing in the valleys.

It is a map—but not one with rigid directions. It's an invitation. To feel. To remember. To come home to yourself.

You'll meet the younger version of me: the girl who survived what she shouldn't have; the woman who tried to build a life from performance and pain; and the soul who finally said, "No more."

You'll hear stories. Receive tools. Be asked to reflect. But most of all, you'll be invited to reconnect with your own sacred curriculum.

This is for the seekers. The sensitive ones. The ones who've always known there was more. The ones who are done pretending. The ones who are ready to live aligned.

If that's you—welcome! Class is now in session. And this time, you're both the teacher and the student, simultaneously.

Let's begin

Chapter 1

Orientation Week: Who the F Am I and Why Did I Enroll?

Before you can make it through any university, you need to show up to orientation. That awkward, sometimes exhilarating, sometimes overwhelming initiation phase where nothing quite makes sense yet—but you know something's beginning. That's what this chapter is: your soul's orientation week.

When I was newly born, I didn't know I had enrolled in this whole Earth School thing. None of us do. But we arrive: Tiny, vulnerable, full of codes and possibilities. Then life begins layering on the lessons—often without a clear syllabus or office hours.

Take a breath.

Let your shoulders drop.

Let your mind soften.

This chapter is about feeling.

Not fixing. Not performing. Not bypassing.

It's about what happens when you stop managing your emotions—and finally meet them, wholeheartedly.

I was born and raised in Puerto Rico. That vibrant, complex island shaped my earliest experiences of beauty, culture, and sensitivity. When I was sixteen, my family moved to Orlando, Florida. It was a culture shock and a rebirth, all at once. That move marked the first time I really began to question who I was—and whether I belonged.

Fast forward a few years: I met my college sweetheart and— nine months into dating—found out I was pregnant. It was one of those unexpected plot twists that reroute your entire life. We got married. I was young, ambitious, and already carrying the weight of "getting it right." We built a marriage that lasted 13 years and ushered a beautiful son into the world.

When my son was just nine months old, he was diagnosed with aggressive leukemia. The world stopped. The curriculum suddenly manifested as survival mode. Miraculously, he lived.

But just two weeks after his diagnosis, my mother was diagnosed with cancer. Three months later, she passed away.

I didn't get to be present with her. I was caring for my son in a hospital room while she was dying in another. That unprocessed grief became a deep scar I carried for nearly a decade. I buried it beneath responsibilities. I buried it beneath performance. I buried it because that's what I thought strength was.

Eventually, the marriage ended. I divorced after 13 years, and with that ending came the slow beginning of my awakening. I dated. I fell into a few toxic relationships. I learned, again and again, what wasn't love.

Then came my second marriage. Short, intense, karmic. One of those cosmic laboratories where unresolved patterns erupt fast and loud. The relational field was dense—entangled in old wounds, fractured loyalties, and dynamics that made harmony nearly impossible.

I walked into a blended family shaped by deep attachments and unspoken pain, where my presence alone disrupted the illusion of control. Some bonds resisted me. Others welcomed me. But the emotional terrain was volatile, and no amount of love could override what wasn't built on mutual respect or readiness.

It was a sacred test of boundaries which I nearly failed—but ultimately passed when I chose myself. And for anyone who's ever felt invisible inside someone else's family system—I see you. I lived that. And I'm still here, whole and blossoming.

That chapter cracked something open. It brought to the surface a truth I could no longer ignore: how much of my life had been shaped by trying to be what everyone else needed. A high-functioning version of me that was slowly burning out.

I had spent over 24 years in construction engineering and project management. I was the strong one. The capable one. The one who held it all together.

But quietly and persistently, I kept switching jobs—every few years, like clockwork.
I'd start out excited, fully committed, telling myself, "This is the one."
And then, something would shift. The cracks would show. The misalignment would speak.

It became most obvious after I left my first marriage. Not long after, I walked away from the job I thought I'd retire from.
That was the moment the pattern began.
From then on, I found myself in a cycle—every two years, I'd

land a new job, feel hopeful… and then slowly realize I needed to leave again.

The pattern was becoming undeniable: I wasn't just switching roles.
I was trying to stay enrolled in a class that my soul had long ago completed: passed with flying colors.

But I was too stubborn to redirect. I kept pushing forward. And so, life kept making it harder—louder and more uncomfortable—until I had no choice but to pay attention, and pivot.

Eventually, I listened. I walked away. From the jobs. From the marriages. From the masks.

And for the first time, I enrolled in the real curriculum:

Self-Love 101. Living Aligned. Embodying Truth.

I wasn't ghosting myself anymore. I was showing up.

So, if you're here wondering who you are and why you came—good. You're exactly where you're meant to be.

Orientation might be messy. But it's sacred.

You don't need to have it all figured out. You just need to be willing to show up.

To notice the patterns.

To listen to the whispers.

To admit what no longer fits.

That's how the real curriculum begins.

Welcome to Week One. Let's begin.

In the chapters ahead, we'll walk together—through the body, the heart, the spiral of healing, and back into joy. You won't just read this book. You'll *live* it. This isn't about concepts. It's about embodiment. It's about reclaiming your place in the classroom of your life.

Chapter 2

Feelings 101: Relearning the Language of Emotions

There should be a damn warning label at the start of this class:

"Feeling your feelings may cause spontaneous breakdowns, deep clarity, unexpected joy, repressed rage, and moments of remembering who you actually are."

Because the truth is, most of us were never taught how to feel.

We were taught how to function.

How to look fine.

How to be nice.

How to perform.

How to tuck our truth away so it wouldn't make anyone else uncomfortable.

But here's the thing: your feelings are not the problem.
Your feelings are the portal.

We don't avoid feeling because we're weak.
We avoid feeling because our bodies remember things that our younger selves were never taught how to fully process, digest, integrate.
And at some point, your nervous system decided that staying in your head was safer than living in your body.

For me, that disconnection started early.
Like so many, I experienced trauma that left imprints on my body and soul.
I dissociated a lot of my childhood.

If that's true for you, too—pause here. Take a breath.
This chapter won't rush you. It will meet you where you are.
Your feelings are not too much. They're how you find your way home.

When the people who are supposed to protect you don't, your body gets the message that safety has to be manufactured.
That control is your only refuge.

So, I learned to be strong. Hyper-independent. High-achieving. Capable.
I built an identity around being unfazed.
Always strong. Always capable.
But inside, I was nowhere to be found. I was emotionally disconnected—numb but functional.

I didn't know how to cry. I didn't know how to rest. I didn't know how to ask for help.
I didn't even know how to locate myself beneath all the layers I had built.

And when my son was diagnosed with cancer—and then just two weeks later, my mother received the same news—I locked it down even more.
His treatment would last six months.
She only made it through three.

I was living in hospital rooms, trying to keep my son alive, while knowing my mother was dying in another.
I buried my grief so deep, I forgot I was even carrying it.
I told myself, "Be strong."
I thought feeling would make me fall apart.
So, I didn't.

Until the mask cracked.
Until life handed me enough wake-up calls that I couldn't ignore the truth anymore.

Feeling didn't break me.
It saved me.

But something eventually broke through.
A moment I didn't expect—yet had been leading toward.

One of the most powerful turning points came during a hypnotherapy session.
I dropped into the subconscious terrain I had spent years avoiding.

I entered the session numb, clenched, unsure if I'd feel anything.
But when I heard those words, my breath deepened.
My chest softened.
It felt like something ancient inside me was finally exhaled.

And what I heard cracked my wide open:

"The more you release your blocks, the more light you let in. Your tears are sacred. Your feelings matter. Say yes to life. Remember—you are magic."

That moment wasn't just emotional.
It was alchemical.

I cried. Not from pain, but from the beauty of finally feeling again.

It was like my body whispered, *Thank you.*

That session awakened the version of me who was ready to come home.

The part that was ready to say:

"I want to be here. I want to feel. I want to live."

So, this chapter is a love letter to your nervous system.

To the part of you that chose survival when it didn't feel safe to stay present.

Your nervous system didn't betray you—it protected you.

But protection isn't the same as peace.

And now your body is ready for a new way.

To the body that held your pain long after your mind forgot.

To the emotions that arise not to destroy you, but to deliver you back to yourself.

You don't have to feel everything all at once.

You just have to stop running from the truth inside of you.

And if you don't know how to begin, here's what I tell my clients:

Start with breath.

Add some stillness.

Let your body speak.

Planet Earth University

Let your tears flow.
And most of all, don't rush the return.

You are safe to feel.
Your body is waiting to be heard.
Are you ready to listen?

This is the real curriculum.
This is where we begin to remember.
Not just what happened—but who you are beneath it all.

Welcome to Feelings 101.
Let's take attendance.

Chapter 2 Bonus Work

Journal Prompts

Feelings 101: Relearning the Language of Emotion

To prepare for this practice, find a quiet, undisturbed space where you can feel safe being fully present. Remember that this is sacred time with yourself—a reunion, not a performance. You may want to use a journal, speak your responses aloud, or even record them as voice notes. There is no right or wrong way to do this. Let your answers flow spontaneously and honestly, without overthinking. Write or speak freely, allow pauses, feel into your body. After you finish, take a moment to re-read or reflect upon what you shared: you may notice new layers of meaning or emotional truths rising to the surface.

Explore the Disconnection

1. When did I first learn that it wasn't safe to feel?

   o What emotion did I learn to hide most?

2. Who did I have to become, in order to survive?

- o   What parts of me were left behind in that process?

3. Where in my life do I still go numb, distract, or override my own body?

The Body Remembers

4. What is my body trying to tell me lately that I haven't been listening to?

5. When was the last time I cried—and did I feel better, or worse, afterward?

6. What's my relationship with rest, softness, and stillness?

The Return

7. If I believed that feeling my feelings would lead me back to myself, what might I finally allow myself to feel?

8. What would it look like to stop ghosting myself?

9. What do I want to feel more of in my life—not in theory, but in my body?

Integration Tools for Reconnection

Use this **mini emotional check-in** anytime you feel disconnected or overwhelmed.

1. Pause. Place your hand on your heart or belly.

2. Breathe in slowly through your nose (count of 4), exhale through your mouth (count of 6), as though saying *"ahh."*. Complete three cycles of this gently extended breathing.

3. Ask yourself:

   "What am I feeling right now?"
   "Where do I feel it in my body?"
   "What does it need from me?"

No fixing. No judgment. Just witnessing.

Release to Peace Practice

This is a gentle, embodied way to process stuck emotion.

1. Find a safe, quiet space where you can be uninterrupted.

2. Begin with 3 slow breaths.

3. Say aloud or silently: "I allow what I've been holding down to emerge. It's now safe to feel these feelings."

4. Place your hand over the area of your body where emotion feels strongest.

5. Move, stretch, cry, shake, sigh—whatever your body wants to do. Let it.

6. When the wave softens, say: "I honor what was felt. I release what no longer serves me. I return to peace."

Repeat as often as needed. It's not about getting rid of or "finishing" the emotion—it's about making space for this energy to move, shift, transform.

Chapter 3

The Pleasure Lab: Reclaiming Joy, Softness, and Sensual Presence

Most of us weren't taught that pleasure was sacred.
We were taught that it was a reward.
Something you had to earn—after the work, the
performance, the sacrifice.

But what if pleasure isn't something you have to earn?
What if it's something you can simply *return* to?

The truth is, reclaiming joy and softness after a life of survival
is its own kind of revolution. And for many of us, pleasure
was buried beneath years of hyper-independence,
overachieving, people-pleasing, and emotional disconnection.

That was true for me.

After decades of performing strength, holding it all together, and building a high-functioning life that looked great on paper, I hit my limit. My nervous system was done: a frazzled mess. My soul was done: waving its white flag of surrender.

And when my second marriage ended—a short, intense, karmic chapter filled with some very advanced relationship labs—I realized: I couldn't keep outsourcing joy anymore.

That was the final wake-up call. The end of the performance. The moment I started choosing *me*.

But the truth is, the whispers (from that quietly wise voice inside) started even earlier. My body had been trying to get my attention long before I was ready to listen.

My Story: The Moment My Body Got Louder Than My Mind

I didn't realize how far I had abandoned myself—until my body made it impossible to ignore.
It didn't whisper.
It roared like a wounded lioness.
Through vertigo, hearing loss, and waves of incapacity, it demanded my attention.
And that's when everything began to change.

There was a point in my life when I could no longer ignore my body.

I was losing my hearing. I had constant vertigo. I was diagnosed with Meniere's disease. The attacks would leave me completely incapacitated. I couldn't even move my eyes or open them without triggering violent vomiting. I couldn't walk.

For hours on end, I would lie utterly helpless and bedridden—until my body regained alignment. At my worst, I couldn't even wipe my own ass. That was the reality. That was how far I had drifted from myself.

The ear-nose-throat specialists—one after another—told me there was no cure. One even suggested they destroy my inner ear nerve to manage the symptoms. Every cell in me said no.

They prescribed anti-anxiety meds. Again—no.

I knew this wasn't just about my ear. I didn't have the language at the time, but I could feel it: my body was screaming, and I hadn't been listening.

My first escape attempt from the jail of corporate-hood and the soul-depleting charade that I had created was in February 2022. I had finally hit my limit, and something in me just said, Go. So, I did. I ended up in San Antonio, Texas, at my dear friend's house. She saw where I was—zombie-like, numb, lost, confused—and suggested that I visit her neurokinetic practitioner.

That session was the beginning of something. A spark. A breath of freedom.

She began working on the extreme tension in my jaw. And during the session, something happened which I'll never forget:

I had a full-body, involuntary release of energy. The rage, grief, pressure I hadn't even known I was holding—locked up in my right jaw—all at once was released: just gone.

It didn't make sense to my mind. But my soul knew: this was truth. This was freedom.

That moment changed me. The symptoms? Gone. The hearing loss? Improved. The story I had lived in—that something was wrong with me—shattered.

Because I finally felt—opened to and intimately encountered—what I had been running from.

That day, I stopped performing and started listening—to my body, my heart, and my own emotional truth.

But the escape from corporate-hood only lasted for six months. The fear crept back in—the old programming, the scarcity, the "what ifs." And before I knew it, I had reenlisted to work again.

I went back.
Not because I wanted to—but because fear still had a voice.
The illusion of safety pulled me in, one paycheck at a time.

I stayed there for another year and a half before I finally broke out for good.

That neurokinetic session had planted the seed, though. It had opened the door to everything that came next. That day, I started feeling and owning my journey.

I had already left the marriage. And now, once again, left the workforce. I left the story that said my worth was based on what I could produce.

And for the first time in my adult life, I asked:

"What does it feel like to be soft? What does it mean to be alive in this body—not just functional, but *free*? What brings me joy?"

It was like learning to breathe again.

I remember taking myself out to lunch alone just to watch the sunlight hit the table. I remember lying in bed with no alarm, just because I could. I remember going for walks without earbuds in, letting the breeze land on my skin like a prayer.

It was uncomfortable at first. Even guilt-inducing. But eventually, it became nourishing. And then... it became *necessary*.

Pleasure, for me, became a portal. Not just to joy, but to embodiment. Not just to sensuality, but to truth.

And eventually, it led me back to my heart.
Because softness isn't just a feeling—it's a frequency.
Joy isn't just emotional—it's spiritual, it's consciousness.
The body led the way, but it was the heart that opened the door.

Because when you let life feel good, you let *yourself* feel real.

You don't need anyone's permission to experience beauty, rest, or bliss. You just need to remember that you're worthy of it.

You always were.

So, if this chapter feels foreign or scary or even a little indulgent... good. That means you're on the edge of remembering something sacred.

This is the part of the curriculum where you don't just process the past—you reclaim the present. You let joy come back online.

You are allowed to feel good.

You are allowed to come alive.

Now, ask yourself:

What forms of pleasure do I deny myself—and why?

Chapter 3 Bonus Work

Journal Prompts: Coming Home to Pleasure

To prepare for this practice, find a quiet, undisturbed space where you can feel safe being fully present. Remember that this is sacred time with yourself—a reunion, not a performance. You may want to use a journal, speak your responses aloud, or even record them as voice notes. There is no right or wrong way to do this. Let your answers flow spontaneously and honestly, without overthinking. Write or speak freely, allow pauses, feel into your body. After you finish, take a moment to re-read or reflect upon what you shared: you may notice new layers of meaning or emotional truths rising to the surface. Now, ask yourself:

1. When was the last time I felt true, soul-deep joy?

2. What forms of pleasure do I deny myself—and why?

3. What parts of me believe I need to *earn* rest, softness, or beauty, rather than simply *claim* them as my birthright?

4. What would it look like to receive pleasure without guilt?

5. How does my body respond when I slow down and breathe?

6. What kinds of experiences make me feel most alive?

7. What daily rituals bring me a sense of presence or peace?

8. If I stopped performing for others, what kind of life would I create?

Pleasure Ritual: The Sacred Yes

The purpose of this pleasure ritual is to reconnect with your body and reclaim the softness, presence, and joy that are your birthright. **What you'll need:**

- a quiet, comfortable space

- a candle, soft fabric, essential oil, or anything that evokes beauty

- a journal or piece of paper

Steps to Creating Your Pleasure Ritual

1. **Set the space.** Dim the lights. Light your candle. Play soft music if you'd like.

2. **Drop into your body.** Place one hand over your heart, the other over your belly. Take three slow, deep breaths. Hear and feel your precious human body being breathed, effortlessly.

3. **Ask yourself:** "What do I want to feel right now? What does my body want in this moment?"

4. **Gently let yourself follow the answers**—whether that's stretching, lying down, dancing, sipping tea, or simply breathing.

5. **Whisper or write this phrase:** "I am allowed to feel good. I am allowed to receive. I am allowed to be soft."

6. **Close the ritual with gratitude.** Thank your body for showing up. Thank your soul for leading you here.

Repeat this ritual anytime you find yourself disconnected from joy. Let it become a sacred act of remembering: *you are not here to survive—you are here to feel.*

Chapter 4

Beauty Appreciation Class: Seeing the Divine in the Mundane

There comes a point in every awakening journey when the healing shifts.

It's no longer just about fixing what's broken—
It becomes about seeing what was always beautiful.

This is that moment.

Beauty is not fluff. It's not decoration. It's not some extra credit on your soul's report card.
Beauty is medicine.
It's a frequency that attunes you to your wholeness.

And when you learn how to see it—in the ordinary, in the messy, in yourself—your whole life begins to bloom.

But oftentimes it takes a breakdown to see beauty clearly.

For me, that moment came on October 20, 2023.
It was my first-time climbing Bell Rock in Sedona.

I had just taken a leap of faith one week earlier—on October 13, I walked away from my old life as an engineer and corporate leader.
I dropped the mask.
I said yes to the unknown.

That climb wasn't just physical—it was spiritual.

I was on a retreat that week, living in sacred space with a group of beautiful souls—including several men who were husbands to powerful, heart-centered women.
Their presence on that mountain was part of my healing.

For years, I had carried subconscious wounding tied to masculine energy—rooted in trauma, betrayal, control, and emotional absence.
But on that climb, I felt something shift.

I was being witnessed, not judged.
Held, not fixed.

The climb got harder the higher we went.

My mind started racing.

My thoughts turned against me—

"You're not strong enough. This is too much. Turn around."

But I wasn't alone.

At the steepest inclines, the men reached out.

They linked their hands and held me by the wrists, pulling me

up when I didn't think I could go any farther.

And they didn't just offer strength—they offered presence.

With every pull, they gave me more than momentum.

They gave me words of affirmation.

They offered encouragement.

They shared their grounded, masculine energy—steady,

reverent, unwavering.

Their support wasn't just physical.

It was emotional.

Energetic.

Multidimensional.

With each step, I was rising not just in elevation—but in

truth.

It was a crescendo—of trust, of surrender, of remembering

what it felt like to be supported without being overpowered.

My soul…
My soul had something else to say.

I kept going. And when I neared the summit of the butte, I
stood in stillness, overlooking the valley below.
And then it happened:

A piercing scream erupted from my body—
Primal, raw, holy.

It came from the depths of my being.
It was rage. It was oppression.
It was years of body shaming, self-betrayal, silencing, and
shrinking.
It was release—not pretty, not polished, but real.

Decades of pressure, perfectionism, holding it all in—gone.

I felt the Earth holding me.

And I wasn't alone.

The same two beautiful, balanced men who had helped me
climb—who held my wrists and pulled me up the steepest
parts—stood nearby now.

Strong. Present. Attuned.

They didn't try to fix me.
They didn't interrupt or look away.

They witnessed.

They held a sacred space so that I could have my moment.
So I could release decades of pain in safety.
So my soul could remember what it felt like to be held, not controlled.

That memory… that frequency… it imprinted something deep within me.
It uploaded a new code of what safety could feel like, moving forward.

I felt my soul expanding.
I saw beauty everywhere.

And the truth is—it had always been there.
I had just been too armored, too busy, too afraid to notice.

Since that day, I've made it a daily devotion to notice beauty—not in grand gestures, but in the subtle.

I began to find it in the steam rising off my tea in the morning, the curve of a tree branch reaching toward the sky, a stranger's unexpected laugh, and even in the sound of my own breath.

These small moments became sacred.
They reminded me that life is always offering softness—if only I'm willing to see it.

Because when you acknowledge beauty,
you remember that you are part of it.

Beauty isn't something you earn.
It's something you notice.
It's something you *receive*.

And when you see beauty, you remember:
"If this moment can be sacred… maybe I can be too."

Chapter 4 Bonus Work

Journal Prompts: The Beauty Between the Lines

To prepare for this practice, find a quiet, undisturbed space where you can feel safe being fully present. Remember that this is sacred time with yourself—a reunion, not a performance. You may want to use a journal, speak your responses aloud, or even record them as voice notes. There is no right or wrong way to do this. Let your answers flow spontaneously and honestly, without overthinking. Write or speak freely, allow pauses, feel into your body. After you finish, take a moment to re-read or reflect upon what you shared: you may notice new layers of meaning or emotional truths rising to the surface. Now, ask yourself:

1. What do I find beautiful that I often overlook?

2. When was the last time I felt awe?

3. What gets in the way of me seeing the beauty around or within me?

4. When was the last time I let myself be witnessed in my truth?

5. What would it mean to live in devotion to beauty?

6. How did I define beauty growing up—and what do I want it to mean now?

7. What would change if I approached life like everything was holy?

Welcoming Beauty: A 5-Minute Ritual

This beautiful ritual can help rewire your nervous system in a way that supports increasing openness to presence, softness, and wonder.

1. Find a quiet spot—either outside or near a window.

2. Take three deep breaths. Let your gaze soften.

3. Slowly scan your environment and *name aloud* five things you find beautiful. It could be light, shape, texture, sound, memory, or even stillness.

4. Let each moment land. Breathe it in.

5. Close your eyes and whisper: "Beauty lives in me, and I am learning to see again."

Repeat daily, especially when life feels dull, numb, or heavy. Beauty is always speaking. Let this ritual help you listen a bit more deeply, so you can hear and lovingly welcome it.

Welcome to the Beauty Appreciation Class. You already passed the test. You just forgot you were made of everything lovely.

Chapter 5

Anatomy of Joy: Healing Through Pleasure, Play, and Presence

There comes a time in your healing when the breath slows.

The body softens.

The ache turns into aliveness.

This is that chapter.

There's a moment in healing when the grief softens.

The stories fade.

And a quiet question arises from within:

What now?

For a long time, I thought the answer had to be *more healing*.
More shadow-work. More unearthing. More fixing. But
eventually, I realized—that loop never ends. The pursuit of
constant repair can become its own cage.

At some point, we don't need to go deeper.
We need to go **lighter**.

You'll intuitively know when that shift is ready to happen—
when your body, your spirit, and your soul are no longer
asking for excavation, but for expansion. You'll know where
to be once you attune to yourself to your own inner guidance:
to that sacred compass in the core of your being.

That's where joy lives.

Not the performative kind.
Not the smiling-through-pain kind.
Not the filtered-for-Instagram kind.

I'm talking about real joy—the kind that sneaks up on you,
bubbles from within, and surprises you in the most ordinary
moments. The kind that reminds you you're not just
surviving…
You're alive!

Joy is the frequency of presence. Of softness. Of now.

And it's not frivolous—it's essential.
Joy rewires your nervous system for safety.
Joy reminds your body that it's allowed to feel good.
Joy lets you know you're no longer in the trauma loop—
you've entered the aliveness loop.

The trauma loop is survival.
The aliveness loop is presence.
It's when you stop bracing for life and start dancing with it.

After decades of hypervigilance, people-pleasing, and
performance, joy felt dangerous to me. It felt foreign. Like
something other people were allowed to have... but not me.

But the more I slowed down—the more I allowed myself to
feel and to notice—the more joy found me. Not in grand
gestures or curated moments, but in the quiet, the subtle, the
overlooked:

It came as I danced alone in my kitchen, music up, heart
open.
It came in the way I laughed at my own thoughts while
cooking.
It came with the wind brushing against my cheek, playful and
soft.
It came when I saw a new leaf sprouting on my baby fig tree.

It came when birds gathered twigs and pine needles from my garden to build their nest: a home crafted from the sanctuary I'd made for myself.

It came in unexpected conversations with strangers while traveling—souls that somehow became friends in the span of a moment.

Joy snuck in through the cracks.

It arrived in the stillness.

It came when I stopped chasing healing and started *living*.

And in 2024, I gave myself a gift I had always postponed:

I let joy guide and inspire the itinerary.

I devoted the year to travel.

To walk. To wander.

To let my body lead me across landscapes I had only seen in dreams.

I returned to Puerto Rico and walked the streets of my childhood in silence. Not a single soul knew I was there. It was a pilgrimage of presence. I didn't go to be seen—I went to see.

As soon as I returned, the Universe whispered again—this time with an invitation to Colombia. Colombia reminded me how **alive** color can feel. How vibrancy lives in the air and the rhythm of the people.

It brought me back to aliveness through rhythm.
It reminded me joy doesn't have to be quiet—it can move, pulse, and sing.

Then came a solo trip to Turkey—a land that felt like a conversation between opposites. Ancient and modern. Spiritual and sensual. Turkey was a dance. A remembering.

In that dance, I remembered how to expand into a space which allowed and celebrated the holding of opposites: I could be both sacred and sensual. Rooted and wild. Turkey helped me stop choosing—
and start becoming…

Japan held me in sacred ritual and stillness. Every step felt like ceremony. Every detail, devotion.

It slowed me down to the frequency of reverence.
I remembered that mindfulness is a form of love.

And Egypt… Egypt initiated a remembrance I couldn't put into words.

That land holds memory in its stones. Sacred stories in its sand.

I didn't just visit—I returned.

Egypt didn't just awaken me—it initiated me.

I felt the ancient stir within my bones.

As if the land had been waiting for me to remember who I was.

I ended the year in a city that had seen many versions of me: Barcelona. A place I once visited in my first marriage. Then again during my first sabbatical—a tender attempt to live in alignment. This time, it felt different. I wasn't trying to escape or prove anything. I was just there. Whole. Present. Me.

The city hadn't changed.

I had.

Each place became a sacred mirror.

Each walk, a conversation with my soul.

And through it all, I healed—

not because I was trying to,

but because I finally made space to **live.**

Joy was in the sunrises over unfamiliar rooftops.

Joy was in my breath as I wandered ancient streets.

Joy was in the silence. The permission. The return.

After years of holding it all together…
this was me—untethered, unmasked, **free.**

So many of us believe we need to be fully healed in order to
feel joy.
But what if it's the other way around?

What if **joy is what helps us heal?**

Joy is not the opposite of emotional or spiritual depth—
It's an expression of it.

When you've touched your pain, met your grief, faced your
patterns—joy becomes a reclamation. A radical act. A living
prayer.

It's not denial.
It's declaration.

"I've survived enough. Now I choose joy."

Let this be your permission slip.
To laugh without apology.
To play without guilt.
To live without waiting.

Welcome to the Anatomy of Joy.

Let it move through you. Let it belong to you.

Let it remind you that you were always meant to feel this free.

You don't need a plane ticket.

You don't need permission.

You just need this moment.

This is your joy.

Welcome home.

Chapter 5 Bonus Work

Journal Prompts: Reclaiming Joy

To prepare for this practice, find a quiet, undisturbed space where you can feel safe being fully present. Remember that this is sacred time with yourself—a reunion, not a performance. You may want to use a journal, speak your responses aloud, or even record them as voice notes. There is no right or wrong way to do this. Let your answers flow spontaneously and honestly, without overthinking. Write or speak freely, allow pauses, feel into your body. After you finish, take a moment to re-read or reflect upon what you shared: you may notice new layers of meaning or emotional truths rising to the surface. Now, ask yourself:

1. What does joy feel like in my body?

2. When was the last time I experienced joy without guilt?

3. What beliefs do I still hold about joy being selfish, unsafe, or too much?

4. What playful moments from childhood do I long to recreate?

5. What would it look like to prioritize joy this week— even in small ways?

6. Where does joy already live in my life that I haven't fully acknowledged?

7. If joy were my compass, where would it lead me next?

Joy Activation Ritual: A 3-Minute Energy Shift

Put on a song that makes your body want to move.
Let go of how it looks. Move with abandon. Wiggle. Stretch. Shake. Laugh.

Close your eyes. Smile from the inside out.
Say aloud: "I am safe to feel joy. I am worthy of delight. I choose life."

Repeat as often as needed.
Joy doesn't need a reason. It just needs your presence.
And right now? You are already enough to receive it all.

Joy Tracker: A 7-Day Practice of Remembering

This is not about perfection. This is about presence.

For the next 7 days, track one moment of joy each day.
It could be subtle—a breeze on your cheek, a sip of tea, a
song, a smile, a laugh.

Example layout (you can journal or draw it):

Day	Moment of Joy	How it Felt in My Body
1		
2		
3		
4		
5		
6		
7		

Let this be your reminder: **Joy lives in noticing.**
Let yourself be surprised.

Build Your Joy Playlist

Music is medicine.
It holds memory, frequency, emotion, and activation.

Your assignment:
Create a Joy Playlist that moves your energy into aliveness.
No rules. Let it be weird, wild, nostalgic, sexy, silly—**you.**

A few prompt ideas to get started:

What songs make me dance without thinking?

What music reminds me of freedom?

What songs did I love before the world told me who I had to be?

Title the playlist something playful or sacred. Return to it when you forget who you are.

This isn't about hype. It's about homecoming.

Chapter 6

Remembering the Magic: From Collapse to Choice

Take a deep breath.

We've traveled through grief, pleasure, beauty, and joy.

Now, we arrive at the moment when everything changes—not through effort, but through consciously empowered choice.

There's a moment on the healing path when everything softens. Not because it's all figured out—but because you finally stop fighting yourself. You stop holding your breath.

You stop pushing. You stop pretending. And you start remembering.

That remembering doesn't always come gently. Sometimes, it arrives as a whisper—a sacred nudge that says, *Come home*. But at other times it erupts like a thunderstorm: shattering every illusion you built just to survive.

For me, it began with collapse.

It was during my second marriage. We had a plan. A spreadsheet. A financial roadmap.
Every cell accounted for. Every formula designed for freedom.

But it wasn't a roadmap.
It was a prison made of logic.
A cage wrapped in certainty.
And my soul was suffocating, clamped and squeezed between the rows and columns.

I wasn't a victim. I had agreed—consciously or unconsciously—to every part of it. Every spreadsheet cell was part of the lesson. And every soul who walked beside me played their role perfectly.

The numbers made sense.
But my soul didn't feel safe.

There was no abuse. No obvious wrongdoing. It just felt *wrong*. Misaligned. Disconnected from truth.

I had built a life that looked good on paper—but betrayed my most essential self, the core of my being.

And the most painful part? I helped construct the very cage I felt trapped in. And then convinced myself that I should be grateful for it.

Under my breath, in a quietly desperate voice, I kept imploring: You can make it work. Just follow the plan. Stick to the timeline. But deep down, I knew: I was ghosting my soul. Again.

And then… the world I knew shattered and dissolved right in front of my eyes.

COVID hit. The systems I had trusted crumbled overnight. My career stopped making sense. My marriage unraveled. The illusion shattered.

And what I saw… I couldn't unsee.

I watched people turn on each other out of fear. I witnessed the fracturing of families—how amidst all the discord they just fell apart. I watched institutions and careers I had poured my energy into reveal their true nature: conditional, hollow, performative.

I was being asked to betray my body, my values, and my truth—just to keep a job. And I finally said:

"What is this nonsense?"
"I'm done."

I dropped out.

Not just from a job or a marriage—but from an entire paradigm. I stepped out of the performance. Out of the version of me who equated responsibility with self-abandonment. Out of the belief that safety requires sacrifice.

And in that collapse, I finally chose me.

It wasn't a breakdown. It was a *breakthrough*.

Because when I let it all fall apart, something real had space to emerge.

I began to feel again. No longer numb. No longer pushing through. No longer pretending.

Instead, *feeling:*
The grief.
The rage.
The ache.
The truth.

It all started to rise to the surface ready to be dealt with piece by piece. And in that rawness, something sacred stirred.

I didn't even know what I wanted anymore. And somehow, that was the most liberating truth of all.

I had lived by five-year plans and perfectly organized spreadsheets. But when someone asked me, what brings you joy? I had no answer. I was clueless.

That moment gutted me. But it also saved me.

Because when you no longer know who you are, you finally get to remember.

And that's when the real journey began.

The next layer came through the sacred plant medicine of ayahuasca.

In that space, I purged darkness I didn't even realize I had been carrying. I remember dancing to the rhythm of the drums, feeling the beat move through my body like lifeblood. The medicine began working its way through me. Then came the purge—not just physical, but energetic. I sat down. Laid back. And released.

What came out into the bucket didn't feel metaphorical. It looked like putrid dark energy: dense, heavy, and viscerally real—like something that had been stored in my body for lifetimes.

We are energy. And when the veil thins, you begin to see it that way. I was watching the accumulated weight of lifetimes leave my body—like a snake shedding its old dry skin.

It wasn't just the purge—it was the permission.
To stop carrying pain that wasn't mine.
To loosen my grip on survival.
To choose truth over performance.
To feel what was real—and let it move.

It was rough. But it was holy. And I was safely and sweetly held—not just by the ceremony, but by the medicine itself.

As I softened into that sacred space, I began to pray. For my son. For my siblings. For my father.

And in the middle of that prayer, I heard it—a direct message from my higher self: "Stop abandoning your soul. It begins with loving and caring for yourself first."

And still, Spirit wasn't done with me.

Later, during a hypnotherapy session, I was visited by the energies of my soul family; and by the loving frequencies of Jesus and Mary Magdalene.

Before I even saw her, I could smell roses and eucalyptus. My senses were greatly enhanced: attuned to something beyond the veil. She was there—not as myth, but as memory. As medicine.

They came to remind me:
That we are divine essence.
That our light is meant to shine, not be dimmed.
That my tears are sacred.
That my feelings matter.

That the more I release, the more light I let in.

That joy is not a reward—it is my nature.

That life is still waiting for me to say yes.

But they didn't just want me to remember their presence.

They wanted me to remember their frequency—to live it, to embody it, and to remind others of it.

So that others, too, could remember the same truth they were awakening in me:

That we are sacred.

That we are love.

That we are never separate from the divine—just invited to remember it again, after a period of playful forgetting.

I cried. Not out of pain—but from the beauty of it all.

The beauty of remembering that I matter.

That my desires are holy.

That magic isn't something I have to earn:

It's what returns when I stop abandoning myself.

And that's what this chapter is really about.

Not the breakdown.

Not the medicine.

Not even the ceremony.

But the choice.

The decision to finally say:
I choose soul over survival.
I choose presence over pretending.
I choose magic—not only the kind from fairy tales, but also
the kind that rises when you finally say:
I choose me.
I choose joy.
I choose life.

And you?
You're allowed to choose too!

You can drop the mask.
Walk away from the cage.
Begin again—not with a plan, but with a truth.

You don't have to earn your magic.
You just have to remember it.

This is your moment.
Your soul is already whispering.

Are you ready to listen deeply, and say yes?

Chapter 6 Bonus Work

Emotional Check-In: The Soul Says…

Close your eyes. Place your hands on your heart. Ask yourself, gently:

- What part of me is asking to be seen today?
- What truth have I been avoiding?
- Where in my life am I ghosting my soul?

Let whatever arises be enough.

Journal Prompts: Awakening to Your Magic

To prepare for this practice, find a quiet, undisturbed space where you can feel safe being fully present. Remember that this is sacred time with yourself—a reunion, not a performance. You may want to use a journal, speak your responses aloud, or even record them as voice notes. There is no right or wrong way to do this. Let your answers flow spontaneously and honestly, without overthinking. Write or speak freely, allow pauses, feel into your body. After you finish, take a moment to re-read or reflect upon what you shared: you may notice new layers of meaning or emotional truths rising to the surface. Now, ask yourself:

1. When in my life have I felt most connected to something greater?
2. What synchronicities have I brushed off that were actually important signs?
3. Where in my life am I still living in survival mode?
4. What does my soul long to experience?
5. What would it feel like to live in alignment with wonder, not worry?

Ritual: The Magic Is Real Practice

To prepare for this ritual you'll need: a quiet space, a candle or item that feels sacred, and your open heart.

1. Light your candle. Say aloud: "Today, I invite my soul to lead."
2. Take three deep slow breaths. Let your energy drop from your head to your heart.
3. Place one hand over your chest. Ask: "What do I need to remember right now?"
4. Free-write whatever comes through. Let your soul speak.

5. Close by saying: "Magic lives in me. And I remember now."

Welcome back. This is your return. This is your arising.

Your soul is no longer waiting in the wings. She's now in the lead.

Chapter 7

The Frequency of Feeling:
Navigating the Map of
Consciousness

We were taught to think.

Think, think, think.

Memorize facts. Follow rules. Stay in line.

Math. Science. Social studies. Repetition without embodiment.

But where was the class on feeling?

Where was the curriculum for emotional intelligence?
For navigating grief, shame, joy, and love?

Where was the guidance for understanding how our frequency shapes our reality?

The truth is—we've been educated to ignore the most powerful force we carry:
Our emotions.

The Map of Consciousness (see Appendix 1) isn't just a chart—
it's a missing piece of our evolution.
It should be taught in every school, starting in Pre-K. All the way to PhD level.

Because without emotional awareness, we become grown adults
who know how to build empires
but don't know how to feel ourselves.

And that's the root of so much pain in this world.

We need to learn the language of emotion.
We need to teach our children how to welcome, regulate, express, and elevate their inner world.
This isn't soft.
This is sacred.

Emotional mastery is the future of human evolution.
And it starts now.

Take a Breath. Begin Again.

Place your hand on your chest.
Now ask yourself: How do I feel right now?
Not what you think. Not what you *should* feel.
Just… what's true.

That's where we begin.

Have you ever felt like certain emotions drain you while others uplift and energize you?

What if emotions weren't just moods, but frequencies— vibrational energies that shape your reality and your personal power?

That's what I discovered when I came across Dr. David Hawkins' Map of Consciousness.
It changed everything.

Emotions as Energy: Understanding the Scale

Dr. David Hawkins, a psychiatrist and spiritual teacher, created a scale to measure levels of human consciousness, using applied kinesiology.
His Map of Consciousness assigns numerical values (1 to 1000) to different emotional and energetic states.

Lower emotions like shame, guilt, fear, and anger constrict and contract our energy.

They drain us.

These are states of **force**—driven by external conditions,
rooted in survival and separation.

Above the frequency of 200, emotions shift into **power**:
including states like courage, neutrality, love, and peace.
These are self-sustaining, empowering, and aligned with truth.

Here's a glimpse into the emotional spectrum:

- **Shame (20)**—where self-hatred hides

- **Guilt (30)**—the weight of unworthiness

- **Fear (100)**—the grip of anxiety and survival

- **Desire (125)**—the hunger for more

- **Anger (150)**—the fire of blame

- **Pride (175)**—the mask of superiority

Then… the shift to higher frequencies:

- **Courage (200)**—the willingness to show up

- **Neutrality (250)**—peace without performance

- **Acceptance (350)**—clarity without resistance

- **Love (500)**—compassion in motion

- **Joy (540)**—expansion

- **Peace (600)**—transcendence

- **Enlightenment (700–1000)**—divine unity, beyond form

The shift from force to power is everything.
And the path begins with awareness.

The Trap of Fear

There's a frequency that keeps more people stuck than anything else.
One that's so deeply wired into our nervous systems that we often confuse it with truth.

Fear.

On the Map of Consciousness, Fear calibrates at 100.
It's not the lowest—but it's one of the most common places people get trapped.

Fear disguises itself as protection.
As logic.
As "just being careful."

But beneath it is a wound—a deep mistrust in life, in self, in Source.

Fear keeps us small.
It says: *Don't speak up. Don't try that. Don't shine too bright. Don't*

get your hopes up.

It convinces us that safety is found in sameness, in silence, in staying in the familiar.

But here's the truth:

Fear is a liar.

It doesn't keep you safe—it keeps you stunted.

It delays your expansion. It shrinks your light. It silences your soul.

And I get it.
I've lived under fear's roof.
The fear of rejection. The fear of being too much. The fear of failing in public.
Even the fear of what might happen *if* things actually worked out.

But I've learned that fear loosens its grip only when you turn and face and lovingly approach it—rather than ignoring or running away from it.

When you breathe through it.
When you name it.
When you remember that you are not the voice of fear—you are the awareness behind it.

Fear loses power when you stop making it the decision-maker.

Because fear is part of the map...
But it's not your home.

You are meant to rise higher.

The Trap of Desire

There's another emotional frequency that often masquerades as ambition or drive—but it quietly keeps us stuck.

Desire.

On the Map of Consciousness, Desire calibrates at 125.
It's higher than apathy, guilt, or fear—but it's still a state of **force**.

Desire can look like motivation. It can even feel exciting at first.
But underneath, it carries a subtle message: *"I don't have enough. I'm not enough. I need something outside of me to feel whole."*

And that's where we get caught.

This is the trap of consumerism.
Of endless scrolling.
Of chasing the next thing, the next title, the next hit of approval.

Desire is what the modern world thrives on.
It's baked into marketing campaigns, hustle culture, and even spiritual bypassing.
We're taught to *manifest more, achieve more, be more*... always *more*.

But the more we chase, the further we get from truth.

Because **Desire is never satisfied**.
It's rooted in the illusion of lack—a hunger that no external thing can feed.

I've lived there too—buying things I didn't need, saying yes when I meant no, confusing visibility with worth.
It took a lot of honesty to see that beneath the striving... was a wound. A longing to be enough.

True power begins when we put the chase on pause.
When we ask ourselves:

"Is this coming from fullness—or from lack?"

When we desire from love, from alignment, from soul—it's clean.
But when we desire from scarcity, fear, or performance— we're just feeding the loop.

The path forward isn't about *having more*.

It's about **feeling more**.

More gratitude. More presence. More truth.

Because nothing outside of you will ever give you what your soul already knows.

The Trap of Pride

There's a tricky emotional state that often gets misunderstood: *Pride*.

It feels better than shame or anger. It offers identity, certainty, even belonging.

But Pride lives in force. It creates separation. It hinges on comparison and performance. It keeps us attached to proving instead of becoming.

And I've been there too—clinging to being right, needing to be validated, building walls instead of softening into truth.

In today's culture, Pride is cleverly packaged—in media, in movements, in influence.

We're made to feel seen… but not liberated.

True power begins when we leave the loop.
When we release identity and step into awareness.

Ask yourself:

Does this uplift me into love, wisdom, and courage?
Or does it keep me needing to defend or be right?

The difference is subtle. But it's everything.

The Breadcrumb That Changed Everything

I discovered the Map of Consciousness during a session with one of the many teachers I've encountered in this Earth school.

She asked me a simple question:
"How are you feeling right now?"

I placed one hand on my heart, one on my abdomen, and I tuned in.

"I feel anger," I said.

She didn't try to fix it. She didn't explain it away.
She simply showed me the Map.

That was it. A breadcrumb.

But it shifted my path entirely.

Once I saw that anger had a frequency—and that I could move *up* that frequency consciously—I felt powerful again. Not because I avoided the anger, but because I honored it.

That's when I understood:

Feelings are energetic signatures.

Emotions are doorways.

And awareness is power.

Final Truth: This Is Consciousness Intelligence

We live in a world that profits from your disconnection.

From your craving. From your reactivity. From your need to prove and perform.

But when you *feel* with awareness—when you begin to name your emotion and choose your next state—you reclaim your life.

You stop performing.

You start transmuting.

You begin to live in the frequency of love.
Of peace.
Of joy.

Not because life is perfect—
But because *your presence is.*

When you master your emotions, you don't control life—you co-create with it.
You become a conscious conductor of frequency.
Not perfect. Not bypassing.

Just awake.

This is how you rise.
This is how you remember.

Chapter 7 Bonus Work

Journal Prompts: Consciousness Intelligence in Action

To prepare for this practice, find a quiet, undisturbed space where you can feel safe being fully present. Remember that this is sacred time with yourself—a reunion, not a performance. You may want to use a journal, speak your responses aloud, or even record them as voice notes. There is no right or wrong way to do this. Let your answers flow spontaneously and honestly, without overthinking. Write or speak freely, allow pauses, feel into your body. After you finish, take a moment to re-read or reflect upon what you shared: you may notice new layers of meaning or emotional truths rising to the surface. Now, ask yourself:

1. What am I feeling right now?
   (Don't censor or edit. Just name what's true.)
2. Where might this emotion sit on the Map of Consciousness?

(Feel into it intuitively. No need to be exact.

Awareness is the win.)

3. What activated this emotion?

   (Was it internal: a memory, belief, thought?

   Or external: a conversation, trigger, or situation?)

4. What emotion am I willing to move toward next?

   (Reach gently for a higher state—not perfection, just

   resonance.)

5. How would it feel in my body to embody that next

   frequency?

   (What would shift in my breath, posture, or energy?)

6. What belief or identity might I need to release to rise?

   (Old stories about worth, safety, love, power—what's

   ready to be released?)

7. What truth am I reclaiming about who I really am?

   (Declare it. Own it. Write it like a mantra from your

   soul.)

Breathwork Ritual: The Breath of Conscious Presence

This practice can be completed in 3–5 minutes. Or longer.
You set the pace.

Create your sacred space.

Sit or lie down. Let your body be supported.

Place one hand on your heart, the other on your belly.

Breathe with intention.

Inhale slowly through your nose.

Exhale gently through your mouth, as though saying *"ahh."*

Repeat three times to come home to yourself.

Name what's here.

Internally or aloud, speak the words: "Right now, I feel ..."

In this way, name the emotional frequency you're now experiencing.

Let it arise. No Judgment. Just truth.

Feel your felt sense.

Breathe into the space between your heart and womb.

Soften any tension, resistance, or constricted sensation.

Reach for resonance.

Name the frequency you're ready to invite in.

Breathe it in, welcoming it fully. And then exhale the old frequency—letting it flow out, liberating it and you.

For instance, with the inhale you might say, "I welcome courage." And with the exhale, "I release fear."

After ten or fifteen repetitions (or more if you'd like) seal the practice with a mantra: "I honor where I am. I know how to rise. I trust my inner compass."

Let this truth guide your next breath, your next choice, your next chapter.

Consciousness Shift Log

You don't need a fancy form to practice frequency elevation. But if you'd like to track your growth over time, I've included a **printable version of the Consciousness Shift Log** in Appendix 2 for you to copy or recreate in your journal.

Use it as a sacred self-awareness ritual: a space to witness your energetic patterns and your own power to shift them. This is your bridge between reactivity and remembrance. It will help you remember:

You are not your triggers.
You are the witness.
You are the transmuter.

Let the map serve as a mirror, not a measurement.
Your frequency isn't a grade—it's a guidepost.
One breath, one awareness, one shift at a time.

Chapter 8

Sacred Truth-Telling: Truth in the Bones

Before we move forward, we must visit what was buried.
This is not an easy chapter—but it is a necessary one.
I invite you to take a breath and meet me here.

Now that we've explored how emotions are energetic
frequencies and how awareness is a key to transformation, it's
time to descend into the place most of us were taught to
avoid: our deeper truth.

This next chapter is not just a story—it's a reclamation. And
it's one I've carried for a long time.

There are some stories that live in the bones.

Stories we carry quietly.

Stories we outgrow before we ever fully understand them.

This is one of those stories.

And while it's my personal story, I want to name this truth clearly:

Sexual trauma does not discriminate.

It can happen to any gender, at any age, in any environment.

No identity protects us from this or any other kind of pain—

And no experience ever lessens our inherent worth.

You may have your own version of this story.

Different details. Same energetic scar.

This chapter is for you, too.

I don't share this for its shock value. I don't share this to garner sympathy.

I share this because it's time.

Because there are too many of us still walking around thinking we have to bear the pain of this alone.

Too many of us still believing that if we just stay quiet, strong, and "healed-looking," maybe the world will stop noticing the frazzled weight we carry in our nervous systems.

But silence doesn't heal shame.
Truth does.

I was sexually abused as a child.
By someone close: a family friend.
Someone I was expected to be polite to.
Someone I had to keep seeing—smiling, performing, staying quiet.
Because that's what little girls are taught to do.

That experience created an energetic split in me.
It hardwired my system for survival.
I became hypervigilant. Controlling. Overachieving.
I built a fortress made of masculine energy and perfectionism.

My body didn't feel like home.
My feelings were locked behind a firewall.
My worth? Tied to achievement and how well I could perform.

Trauma disconnects us from the body.
It makes us freeze, flee, or fragment.
But healing brings us back—
To breath. To presence.
To the sacred space between heart and womb.

That's where my truth now lives—and where I continue to
listen.

Years passed. I excelled on the outside.
But inside, I was fractured.
And then life handed me the perfect storm:
My second marriage.

It was a pressure cooker.
Intense. Emotional. Unrelenting.
Karmically designed to crack me open.

I started reacting in ways that shocked even me.
I'd spiral into rage over small things, and I couldn't
understand why.

I remember one argument where I completely lost it.
My ex-husband looked at me like I was someone else—
because, in a way, I was.

It wasn't adult me who was reacting.
It was Little Jessica.
The one who had never screamed.
The one who had never cried out.
The one who had been silenced when it happened.

At some point in that marriage, I told him.
I opened up about the abuse.
But he wasn't emotionally equipped to receive, hold, and
provide a safe harbor for it.
He heard the words, but they never truly landed.
And I was left, once again, carrying the weight alone.

Still, when it's time to heal, the soul keeps nudging.
I reached out to a therapist (virtually) because I needed help
navigating the emotional chaos of the marriage.
And yet, it was in that remote, pixelated space that the thread
was finally pulled.

That's when I realized:
This pain hadn't gone anywhere.
It was still living inside me.
Buried beneath years of pretending.

My inner child—still raging, still frozen—had been waiting.

The unraveling had begun.

But even with that awareness, I didn't know what it meant to
feel truly supported... until the chakra reset retreat.

It was a weekend immersion into the full energetic body.
Root to crown.

We moved through all the chakras—one by one—clearing
what no longer served, activating what had been dormant,
and opening channels that had long been closed.

During a powerful kundalini sequence, something ancient
inside me broke open.
I began to cry—loud, guttural, primal sobs.

And this time… I wasn't alone.

I was held. Witnessed. Honored.

The facilitators didn't flinch. They didn't interrupt.
They paused the entire class so I could catch my breath.
They let me cry. Let me be seen. Let me unravel.

One by one, others shared their stories too.
It wasn't just *my* healing—it became a *collective return*.

That moment—being seen in my pain and still belonging—
It changed something fundamental in me.
It showed me what real support feels like.

From there, the next wave of healing came through
hypnotherapy.
And then—deeper still—through a Quantum Healing
Hypnosis Technique (QHHT) session.

In that session, I traveled through lifetimes.
I retrieved healing from other versions of myself.
And at the very end—when I least expected it—
She appeared.

Little Jessica.
Not shy. Not silent.
Angry as hell.

She screamed. She raged.
At the perpetrator. At her family. At the entire world.
And I let her.

That was the day she stopped hiding.
The day her roar was finally heard.

And just as she let her pain emerge and rise like fire,
something extraordinary happened:

A dragon appeared.

My spirit animal.
A sacred ally.
He didn't come to scare me—he came to remind me of who
I am.

That fire isn't only for destruction—it's for alchemy.

He came to show me I was strong.

That I was never alone.

That I was sovereign, fierce, and finally ready to rise.

We burn through feelings not to escape them, but to liberate them.

That day, the fire within me wasn't rage—it was remembrance.

Since I was a child, I believed in magic.

Dragons. Fairies. Other realms.

And now I understand why.

Children are the wisest transmuters of all.

Have you ever watched a child throw a tantrum?

They cry. They scream. They tremble.

And then…

They nap.

They laugh.

They return to joy.

That's transmutation.

We are meant to feel.

We are designed to alchemize.

So, if someone tells you, "I was abused"—
Please don't shrink.
Don't analyze. Don't try to fix it.
Just say: "I see you. I'm sorry you went through that. I'm here."

That's it. That's everything.

And if it's too much for you to hold, that's okay.
Just don't leave them alone with it.
Guide them toward help.
Let them know they deserve support.

Because healing is layered.
It's multidimensional.
It lives in the subconscious.
In the body.
In the auric field.
In the soul.

We are not just physical beings.
We are temples.
We are galaxies.

So, we must heal on all these levels:
Through hypnotherapy. Through somatic massage.

Through movement, breath, and sacred witnessing.
Through love.

We are limitless in our ability to heal.

So, take your time.
Give yourself grace.
Breathe. Cry. Roar. Rest.

You don't have to do it all at once.
You just have to be willing to feel.
To trust that your truth is not too much.
To take the first sacred step toward your own return.

You've got this.

Chapter 8 Bonus Work

Journal Prompts: Truth as Liberation

To prepare for this practice, find a quiet, undisturbed space where you can feel safe being fully present. Remember that this is sacred time with yourself—a reunion, not a performance. You may want to use a journal, speak your responses aloud, or even record them as voice notes. There is no right or wrong way to do this. Let your answers flow spontaneously and honestly, without overthinking. Write or speak freely, allow pauses, feel into your body. After you finish, take a moment to re-read or reflect upon what you shared: you may notice new layers of meaning or emotional truths rising to the surface. Now, ask yourself:

1. What truths have I been afraid to speak aloud?
2. What parts of me still believe I need to protect others from my truth?
3. Where have I abandoned my own voice?
4. What does my inner child still need to feel safe?

5. How does my body want to be heard, honored, or held today?

Ritual: Sacred Self-Witnessing

For this ritual you will need: a mirror, a private space, and a few uninterrupted minutes.

1. Sit or stand in front of a mirror. Gaze into your own eyes.
2. Place a hand on your heart or womb space.
3. Speak these words: *"I see you. I hear you. I believe you. And I will never leave you again."*
4. Welcome any emotions that arise. Let the silence be a container. Let your presence be the medicine.

Repeat as often as needed. This is not about fixing. This is about witnessing.

You are the sacred space you've been waiting for. And you are so worthy of your own truth.

You always were.

Chapter 9

When Survival Looks Like Love: Rewriting the Blueprint of Relationship

Some patterns don't begin in adulthood. They begin in the nervous system. In the body. In the silence between what happened and what was never said.

After the trauma of childhood abuse, I developed an invisible script—one I didn't even realize I was performing, until much later. It wasn't just what happened to me that shaped my relationships. It was what I learned from the absence. From the suppression. From the energetic imprint that said love is earned, safety is conditional, and being chosen means enduring. Those beliefs lived in my body long before they ever lived in my mind.

I didn't walk into toxic relationships because I didn't know better. I walked into them because, at a subconscious level, they felt familiar. Familiar chaos. Familiar emotional unavailability. Familiar silence. It wasn't that I was "attracted" to these dynamics—it's that my nervous system had been wired to believe that love equals tension, inconsistency, or performance. That a partner who ignores me is one I need to try harder for. That if I just love them enough, fix them enough, give enough… maybe I'll be enough.

But that pattern? That's not love. That's survival. And survival isn't sovereignty.

For years, I found myself in relationships that mimicked the very wounds I hadn't yet healed. I was drawn to emotionally unavailable men who couldn't meet me in presence, because that dynamic—that chronic unavailability—mirrored the emotional distance I had experienced in childhood. I stayed in situations that kept me locked in cycles of hope, confusion, and collapse—chasing the high of authentic connection while at the same time bracing for the crash of neglect.

I felt most seen when I was performing, helping, rescuing—because that was when love had always seemed most accessible to me. Each relationship felt like it had potential. Each one felt like maybe this time it would work. And when it inevitably unraveled, I told myself the same story: *"They just weren't ready."*

But the truth was, I wasn't ready either.

I wasn't ready to stop chasing patterns that felt like home—because I hadn't yet created, within myself, a new internal home of safety. I was still carrying—within my subtle body, my emotional field—the energetic blueprint of neglect.

I had confused longing with love.
I had mistaken inconsistency for chemistry.
I had normalized pain-and-reward cycles because my nervous system was trained to expect them.

And in a strange way, those toxic relationships gave me a sense of purpose. If I could work for love—if I could fix, improve, and earn it—then I didn't have to feel the grief of never having truly received it.

And then, the shift began—not all at once, but unmistakably.

It wasn't until I began doing deep subconscious healing—through hypnotherapy, breathwork, family constellation therapy, acupuncture, and energy medicine—that I could finally name the truth: I wasn't chasing love. I was chasing relief. I was chasing the feeling of finally being enough.

Awareness of this truth was the first step. But embodiment—that was the real shift. And it didn't arrive in one perfect moment. It came slowly, subtly, and quietly.

I started listening to my body when it tensed up around someone's energy. I stopped ignoring the red flags that I used to explain away or romanticize. I chose solitude over inconsistency—over the hot-and-cold dynamics that used to leave me anxious and confused. I stopped needing chaos to feel alive.

I began recognizing that the people who once felt exciting to my habitual trauma-cycle now felt dysregulating—and the ones who once seemed boring to my nervous system began to feel peaceful to my soul.

I finally had the capacity to choose peace.

I let go of the addiction to being needed.
I let go of relationships where my presence was only valued

when I was rescuing someone from themselves.
I stopped bending into versions of me that could be more
lovable, more accommodating, more useful.
I stopped outsourcing my worth.

I realized that love isn't earned. It's received.
It's not about proving. It's about remembering.

And for the first time in my life, I stopped reaching outside
of myself to be chosen.
I chose me.

That's when the real love story began—not the one society
writes, but the one my soul had been waiting for all along.
The love story where I became my own safe space.
Where I reparented the inner child who thought she had to
perform to be loved.
Where I held the parts of me that believed love had to be
hard, that intensity meant intimacy, that pain was passion.

I stopped confusing survival strategies for sacred connection.
Because that's not love. That's a pattern.
And patterns—once seen—can be broken.

Now that I am consciously aware… now that I've walked
through my shadows… now that I've remembered who I am

and reconnected with what brings me joy… I know the love I seek starts with me.

I love myself fully. And every day, I work on loving myself unconditionally.
I date myself. I laugh with myself. I hold space for my emotions.
I extend grace to my own process.
I celebrate the woman I've become.

And from this joy—from this grounded, sovereign, whole-hearted place—my energetic field opens.

I now feel ready to attract someone who lives in this consciousness too. Someone who meets me soul to soul.
Not someone looking to be completed, but someone who is already whole. Already anchored.
A partner who desires to walk beside me, not carry or be carried.
A partner for this Planet Earth University. A study partner.

I now call in someone who knows who they are.
Someone emotionally available. Spiritually attuned. Rooted in every chakra, from safety to surrender.
A being who is playful and grounded, creative and calm—balanced in both their softness and their strength.

They are at home in their own skin.

They are not afraid of the work.

They don't avoid the uncomfortable.

They're not afraid of the soul's tutoring sessions. In fact,
they'll retake the class, if needed.

Stay up late to study truth. They are curious. Committed.
Conscious.

And I—I have become that kind of student.

And that is who I now attract.

I've become a sacred mirror—and now I attract one too.

Chapter 9 Bonus Work

Journal Prompts: Recognizing & Rewriting the Pattern

To prepare for this practice, find a quiet, undisturbed space where you can feel safe being fully present. Remember that this is sacred time with yourself—a reunion, not a performance. You may want to use a journal, speak your responses aloud, or even record them as voice notes. There is no right or wrong way to do this. Let your answers flow spontaneously and honestly, without overthinking. Write or speak freely, allow pauses, feel into your body. After you finish, take a moment to re-read or reflect upon what you shared: you may notice new layers of meaning or emotional truths rising to the surface. Now, ask yourself:

1. What relationship patterns have I repeated that mirror old wounds?
2. What did my nervous system associate with love growing up?
3. Where have I mistaken intensity for connection?

4. What would emotional safety feel like in partnership?

5. Who am I when I stop trying to fix, earn, or chase love?

Embodiment Practice: Resetting the Nervous System in Love

For this practice you'll need: a quiet space, your breath, and your intention.

1. Sit or lie down in stillness. Place one hand on your heart, one on your lower belly.

2. Close your eyes. Take three deep breaths in through the nose, then out through the mouth, as though saying *"ahh."*

3. Say aloud or silently:

   "I release the need to chase what isn't mine."
   "I choose peace over performance."
   "I call in love that honors my essence, not my effort."

4. Breathe into this new frequency. Let your body feel the difference.

5. Anchor with this final whisper: "I am the one I've been waiting for."

Chapter 10

Integration: The Return to Wholeness

Healing is not a destination.

It's not a fixed point in time where everything clicks and you're finally "done."

It's a spiral. A deepening. A remembering.

This chapter is about that sacred space in between—the place where you're no longer stuck in survival mode, but you're also not engaged in performative healing. You're just... living. In presence. In truth. In your body. With your soul.

Integration is where it all lands.

It's the walk after the release.

The tea after the cry.

The breath after the breakthrough.
It's not flashy. It's not loud. But it's holy.

Because this is where you become who you've been becoming.

For me, integration looked like creating a life where my nervous system felt truly safe—rather than constantly activated, bracing, or performing.
Safety became my new compass. I no longer mistook adrenaline for purpose.
I prioritized environments, people, and habits that let my body exhale.
I started choosing peace over productivity, and calm over chaos.

It also meant choosing work and relationships that nourished me instead of depleting me.
I stopped over-giving. I stopped proving.
I let reciprocity become the standard.
If something drained me, I released it.
If someone couldn't meet me in presence, I stopped shrinking to stay.
My energy became sacred—and I began protecting it like the precious life-force that it is.

Integration invited me to take walks without a destination.

For most of my life, I was driven by outcomes and to-do lists.

But integration taught me the power of wandering. Of

slowness. Of being in communion with the now.

Those walks became prayer. Movement without pressure.

Stillness in motion.

I learned how to let the moment lead.

It looked like letting my body rest without guilt.

Rest used to be something I had to earn.

Now, it's sacred. A necessity. A way I honor the temple I live

in.

I no longer override my body to match the world's urgency.

I've re-learned how to listen—and to respond with

compassion and grace.

And, perhaps most beautifully, integration looked like

laughing again—

not because the pain was gone,

but because I was no longer afraid to feel.

Joy doesn't mean everything is perfect.

It means I've expanded my capacity to feel the full spectrum.

I can laugh with tears still drying.

I can grieve and still feel light.

I no longer gatekeep joy—I welcome it home.

Integration is when healing leaves the therapy room and enters your daily life.

It's when you stop seeking permission to be whole.

It's when you *fully embody* what used to be only a concept.

And then, as integration deepened, it began offering me sacred reflections. Two moments, in particular, revealed how far I'd come.

One was deep, spiritual, and wholly unexpected.

The other, quietly human.

The first was during a breathwork session. I had been working through a sense of heaviness, breathing through what felt like the weight of lifetimes.

I dropped into a trance-like state, and suddenly I was transported into a scene I didn't expect.

The person who had once violated me—the abuser from my childhood—appeared before me in spirit form.

But not as a monster.

As an angel.

He looked at me and said gently:

"Keep breathing. You're clearing out the old beliefs—the ones that made you feel unworthy."

That moment shattered something. Not because it excused
the harm, but because I finally understood:
My soul wanted freedom more than it wanted punishment.

And in that moment, I let in more light: dissolving a good
part of the darkness.
That didn't mean what happened was okay. It meant I was
okay now.

The second moment was simpler, but just as profound.
I met a friend for dinner and drinks.
As soon as I saw her, I felt her aura—tight, sharp, guarded.
Like a porcupine.
And in that moment, I realized: That used to be me.

I used to walk through the world with my spikes out.
Bracing for the worst.
Protecting from a past that had already passed.

But that night, I wasn't the porcupine. I was the presence.
And that was the sign.
It was subtle. But in my body, I knew that I had crossed into
something new. Something free.

Integration doesn't always announce itself.
Sometimes, it just shows up as who you are no longer.
And who you've finally become.

You don't have to chase awakening anymore.
You are the awakening.

And the more you trust the process—the seasons, the spirals,
the softness—the more you realize:
You've already arrived.

You're not broken. You're not behind.
You're blossoming—exactly as you're meant to.

Welcome home.

You don't have to strive.
You don't have to seek.
You are already home—in yourself.

Chapter 10 Bonus Work

Journal Prompts: Living the Integration

To prepare for this practice, find a quiet, undisturbed space where you can feel safe being fully present. Remember that this is sacred time with yourself—a reunion, not a performance. You may want to use a journal, speak your responses aloud, or even record them as voice notes. There is no right or wrong way to do this. Let your answers flow spontaneously and honestly, without overthinking. Write or speak freely, allow pauses, feel into your body. After you finish, take a moment to re-read or reflect upon what you shared: you may notice new layers of meaning or emotional truths rising to the surface. Now, ask yourself:

1. What does integration mean to me—physically, emotionally, spiritually?

2. In what aspects of my life have I begun living my healing instead of chasing it?

3. What small rituals support my groundedness and truth?

4. Where am I still waiting for permission to rest, feel, or be?

5. How can I honor this chapter of my journey—not by *doing* more, but by more fully and authentically simply *being*?

Ritual: The Embodied Yes

For this ritual you'll need: a quiet space, your breath, and your precious human body.

1. Sit or lie down in stillness. Close your eyes. Inhale deeply.

2. As you exhale, whisper: "I say yes to now."

3. Place one hand on your heart and one on your belly. Feel your aliveness.

4. Repeat: "I am not who I was. I am who I choose to become. I trust the journey. I trust myself."

5. Stay here as long as you need.

This is your integration. This is your homecoming. This is your embodied yes. And it is enough.

Chapter 11

The Art of Living Aligned

Living aligned isn't about perfection.

It's about presence.

It's about truth.

It's about coming back to yourself over and over again—
especially when the world tries to pull you in every direction
but your own.

This chapter is your invitation to live your life as a sacred
yes—not just in your rituals, but in your everyday reality.
Not just in your meditations. But in your money. Your
boundaries. Your pleasure. Your voice.

Alignment is the moment when your inner world and outer
world stop fighting—and begin their sacred dance.
It's when what you believe and how you behave finally
match: mutually support and mirror-image one another.
It's when your nervous system sighs and says:
"Yes—this feels like me."

From Performance to Presence

For a long time, I didn't know what alignment felt like.
I was so used to shape-shifting, code-switching, and
overperforming that I didn't even notice how many of my
yeses were really nos.

Living aligned asked me to unlearn everything I thought
made me worthy.
I had to release the belief that I had to prove myself in order
to be loved.
That constant busyness meant I was important.
That saying yes would keep me safe.
That setting boundaries meant I'd be rejected.
That joy was something to be earned.

These weren't just thoughts—they were survival strategies.
But as I began softening into alignment, I realized that they
no longer served me.

They belonged to the version of me who was still trying to be enough.

And I was finally ready to let her rest.

I remember the day I finally walked away from my engineering career—the title, the steady income, the performance-driven life.

On paper, it looked perfect. But inside, I was exhausted.

My nervous system was fried.

My soul was whispering—and then screaming—*this is not who you are anymore!*

Leaving that life wasn't easy. It was messy. Uncertain. Terrifying.

But it was the first true yes I had given myself in years.

That decision cracked something open.

I stopped outsourcing my identity to roles, titles, and the need to prove.

I began choosing peace over productivity. Alignment over approval.

It looked like saying no to projects that didn't honor my energy.

Letting go of people who only loved the polished version of me.

Trusting my own voice—even when it trembled.
Laughing. Resting. Traveling the world without apology.
Letting joy back in.

That's when I realized: alignment isn't something you earn.
It's something you remember. And reclaim. Again and again.

The Unlearning

That reclamation came with its own initiations.
I had to let go of so much—friendships that no longer
reflected my values, roles I had outgrown, even the illusion of
stability.
I had to grieve the version of me that had built an entire life
oriented around survival and strategy.

There were seasons of deep solitude.
I became a hermit by choice.
Not because I was broken—but because my spirit needed
deep stillness and quietude to recalibrate.
I wasn't isolating. I was incubating.
Making space for the woman I was becoming.

Trusting this process—the unknown, the silence, the letting
go—

that was the real curriculum.

That was living aligned.

Alignment Is a Practice, Not a Performance

Alignment is built in the moment you speak your truth even when your voice shakes.

It's honored when you rest without guilt.

It's embodied when you walk away from what doesn't feel like home—even if it looks perfect on paper.

This life… this sacred curriculum of Planet Earth University…

It's not asking you to get it all right.

It's asking you to get real.

To live in alignment is to become the most honest version of yourself.

Not the most palatable.

Not the most polished.

The most present.

The most connected.

The most *you*.

And when you live from that place, everything aligns.
Not instantly. Not always comfortably.
But authentically.

There is nothing more magnetic than a human being fully anchored in who they are.

You Become a Living Invitation

This is the art of living aligned. This is your final course.
And you already have everything you need to pass.

But just like in life, the learning never really ends.
Each day—each chapter—brings a new lesson.
Class continues.

And thankfully, I'm a much better student now—
in fact, I've become a tutor.
A guide.
A hypnotherapist walking others home to themselves, just as I've done for myself.

Who knows… maybe I'll even go for a master's degree in embodied truth.

One choice, one breath, one sacred yes at a time.
You are your own permission slip.

Chapter 11 Bonus Work

Journal Prompts: Defining Your Aligned Life

To prepare for this practice, find a quiet, undisturbed space where you can feel safe being fully present. Remember that this is sacred time with yourself—a reunion, not a performance. You may want to use a journal, speak your responses aloud, or even record them as voice notes. There is no right or wrong way to do this. Let your answers flow spontaneously and honestly, without overthinking. Write or speak freely, allow pauses, feel into your body. After you finish, take a moment to re-read or reflect upon what you shared: you may notice new layers of meaning or emotional truths rising to the surface. Now, ask yourself:

1. Where in my life do I feel most aligned right now?
2. Where do I feel the most dissonance between who I am essentially, and how I show up?
3. What are the signs my body gives me when I'm out of alignment?

4. What beliefs am I ready to release in order to live more truthfully?

5. What does it look like to live aligned in my work, love, money, and daily choices?

Ritual: The Alignment Audit

For this ritual what you'll need is: your journal, a pen, and some uninterrupted space.

1. Draw a line down the center of a blank journal page.
2. Title the left side, "Aligned" and the right side, "Out of Alignment."
3. Without judgment, begin listing where in your life you feel each energy.
4. Ask yourself: "What would it take to shift one thing from the right side to the left?"
5. Choose one such newly aligned action or activity— and commit to taking this action within the next 24 hours.

Your alignment doesn't live in the big moments.
It lives in your next choice.
And your next one after that.

Keep choosing. Keep coming home.
You're doing it.

**Alignment isn't a goal to reach—it's a truth to
remember.**
Every day, you're coming home.

Chapter 12

Living the Spiral:
When Growth Isn't Linear

Healing doesn't happen in straight lines.
It's not a ladder. It's a spiral.

You don't just "move on." You move inward.
You revisit the same themes, the same wounds, the same
stories—but from a new level of consciousness each time.
You arrive differently, with more truth in your bones, more
softness in your heart.

At first, this can feel frustrating. Like, *"Seriously? This again?"*
But then you realize... this isn't failure. It's refinement.
It's the spiral of evolution.

Healing in Cycles, Not Timelines

There were so many moments I thought I had "healed"
something—only to bump into it again when life got louder.
But I wasn't the same woman.
The me who returned to those wounds was wiser. Gentler.
More honest.
More willing to sit with the discomfort without making it
mean I was broken.

Living in the spiral means honoring the layers—
not rushing to peel them off,
but learning from each one as it reveals itself.

It means recognizing that triggers are not enemies;
they are invitations calling us deeper into ourselves.

Tears aren't signs of weakness—they are sacred thresholds,
gateways into the truth that lives beneath the surface.
Breakdowns become unexpected teachers,
ushering in clarity, surrender, and growth.

And when familiar patterns resurface, it doesn't mean we've
failed—it means we're ready to meet those lessons with more
presence, more softness, and more truth than ever before.

There was a time when I saw myself spinning in circles, stuck
in loops.
Now I see that, in truth, I was spiraling—inward, upward,
deeper.

A Day That Changed Everything

I'll never forget March 28, 2025—the day I gave it all back.

I was in an acupuncture session with someone I had met in
Egypt—a soul connection, a powerful healer.
I didn't expect anything profound to happen. But healing
doesn't ask for permission: It arrives when it's ready.

She placed needles throughout my body, and everything was
calm—until she touched one spot on my upper right arm.
A sharp, soul-deep ache pierced through me.

That's the thing about the body—it never lies. When it hurts
like that, you listen.

She held space while I dropped in.
My third eye opened, and suddenly, I saw a vision: a bloodied
warrior, intense and heavy. Wielding a sword.
The wounded masculine within me—overcompensating,
overprotective, exhausted.

I breathed. I cried. I let him go.

Then she moved to the same point on my left arm.
This time, a different vision: a radiant Druid priestess—
silenced, repressed, aching to rise and speak her truth.

I wept for her too.
I released her.
I set her free.

Releasing the Contract

Then something shifted.
Something bigger than me.

I felt the full weight of all I had been carrying—not just my
own wounds, but the ancestral ones.
The karmic patterns. The pressure to heal it all. To be the one
who broke every chain.

And I heard my soul speak:

"You've done enough. You can let it go now."

So, I did.

I whispered a prayer of release:

*Thank you to my ancestors. To every past life. I honor you. I see you. I
release you. I give it all back—with love and reverence.*

That was the day I broke the contract.
That was the day I chose to spiral forward—not in service of
the past, but in devotion to the now.

What the Spiral Has Taught Me

The spiral is not just a metaphor—it's a sacred geometric shape, consistent across evolutionary cycles and found everywhere in nature:
in galaxies, seashells, the swirl of weather systems, and the helix of our DNA.
It reflects how we grow—not in straight lines, but through sacred cycles of return.

Healing doesn't follow a linear path. It flows in spirals.
Not because you're broken. But because you're ready to meet yourself again—more fully.

You will revisit old wounds. You will feel familiar emotions. You might whisper, *"Haven't I already healed this?"*—but the version of you asking is not the same one who first lived it.

This time, something's different.
You feel deeper. You soften sooner. You choose more truth. You stay present—without abandoning yourself.

That's the spiral. Not regression. Refinement.

Every return offers a new vantage point.
Each cycle invites a wiser, gentler version of yourself, going forward.

It's like climbing a spiral staircase—you may pass the same view again, but from a new height, with new understanding.

So, when the tears revisit, when the old pattern reappears—don't shame yourself.
Honor the spiral.

It means you're still in the sacred curriculum.
Still becoming.
Still remembering.

Living the spiral means I no longer chase perfection.
I honor progress—even when it looks like stillness.
I witness patterns—not with shame, but with curiosity.
I revisit old wounds—not because I failed, but because I'm ready to meet them as the woman I am now.

This isn't about fixing.
This is about remembering.
Again and again.

So, the next time an old story resurfaces… don't judge it.
Witness it.
Welcome it.

And ask:

"What version of me is being invited forward now?"

That's the spiral.

That's the curriculum.

That's the art of living aligned.

And when it spirals back around again—you'll be ready.

Chapter 12 Bonus Work

Journal Prompts: Witnessing Your Sacred Spiral

To prepare for this practice, find a quiet, undisturbed space where you can feel safe being fully present. Remember that this is sacred time with yourself—a reunion, not a performance. You may want to use a journal, speak your responses aloud, or even record them as voice notes. There is no right or wrong way to do this. Let your answers flow spontaneously and honestly, without overthinking. Write or speak freely, allow pauses, feel into your body. After you finish, take a moment to re-read or reflect upon what you shared: you may notice new layers of meaning or emotional truths rising to the surface. Now, ask yourself:

1. In what ways has my healing journey been nonlinear?

2. What themes or patterns do I find myself revisiting—again and again?

3. Do I judge myself for returning to things I thought I had already "healed"?

What if this is actually evidence of deeper mastery?

4. How has my understanding of these patterns changed over time?

5. What lesson or gift am I reclaiming with more depth this time around?

6. What part of me is returning home now?

Embodied Spiral Practice

This beautiful somatic ritual can be engaged with either standing or sitting in a chair or on the floor.

1. Close your eyes. Place one hand over your heart and one over your womb or abdomen.
2. Begin to slowly rotate your body in a spiral motion— gently, intuitively. Let your torso move in circles as small or large as you feel called.
3. With each circle, repeat silently or aloud: *"I honor the spiral. I trust my return. I rise again—wiser, softer, clearer."*

4. Complete at least five slow spirals before reversing the direction.
5. As you finish, settle into stillness. Feel the energy in your body. Anchor in a breath.

Spiral Map of Return

Consider drawing your spiral journey as a **visual map of return.**

You can use this prompt in your journal, sketchbook, or print the template included in Appendix 3.

Start at the center—your origin point. Each loop outward represents a season, shift, or return to a pattern with new awareness.

Label the loops with:

- What surfaced (emotion, story, trigger)
- What you learned or remembered
- A phrase or frequency you claimed

Let this map remind you: Healing is not a straight line.
You are not back at the beginning.
You're rising in rings of ever-more-refined knowing.

Chapter 13

Embodied Leadership:
The Art of Living Aligned

Living aligned isn't about perfection. It's about presence.
The kind that fills a room quietly and changes everything—
not because it's loud, but because it's real.
It's about coming back to yourself over and over again—
especially when the world tries to pull you in every direction
but your own.

There comes a moment on the healing journey where the
work turns outward.
Not because you've "arrived," but because you've integrated
enough to hold space for others.

This isn't about being perfect. This is about being *present*.
This is what I call **embodied leadership**.

True leadership doesn't demand the spotlight.
It radiates quietly—through consistency, through truth,
through how you show up when no one's watching.
It's built on integrity, not image.
Resonance, not performance.

There was a time I led from survival—from the mask, from
the muscle, from needing to prove.
Now, I lead from stillness.
From presence.
From truth.

Embodied leadership means you no longer outsource your
knowing.
You speak when moved, not to be heard.
You set the tone by *being* the tone.
You walk your talk without needing applause.
You remember that the way you live is the medicine.

It's not about a title. Or a platform. Or how many followers
you have.
It's about how deeply you've met yourself—and how willing
you are to meet others from that same place.

The First Sacred Yes

I never set out to be a guide.

But when you do the work, when you walk the spiral, when you come back to your body, your truth, your soul—people feel it.

They recognize something in you. And eventually, they ask:

"How did you do it?"

That's when you know it's time to teach and guide.

Not from a pedestal—but from the spiral.

From the wounds you've touched and the wisdom you've received.

From the embodiment of your own curriculum.

Because when you become a living transmission of your truth—

you give others permission to do the same.

This was the moment I said my first sacred yes.

Not to a role. Not to a performance.

But to being seen—in my fullness, my humanity, my presence.

Performance vs. Presence

This world doesn't need more influencers.

It needs initiators.

Guides who've walked through their own fire—and now carry water for the next wave.

That's what I've become. A tutor in Planet Earth University.
Not because I'm finished—
but because I've remembered enough to help others
remember, too.

Performance taught me how to be liked.
Alignment taught me how to be loved—for who I actually
am.

Anchored. Willing. Ready.

So, if you're feeling the call to lead, but are not sure if you're
ready—
Let this be your sign:

You don't have to be perfect.
You just have to be honest.
Anchored.
Willing.

Every boundary, every pause, every truth became part of my
yes.

Like that moment when I stepped away from proving and
into presence—
when I realized that being honest about my own spiral, my
own healing,
was what gave others the courage to do the same.

That was when I became a leader without needing a title.

Because that's the kind of leadership that changes lives.
That's what creates ripples.
That's what builds new worlds.

And for me, that ripple began the moment I chose to lead
from embodiment—not from ego—
and stepped fully into my role as a tutor in Planet Earth
University.

From within.
From truth.
From the core of my being.

Because in the end, embodied leadership isn't earned—
it's remembered.
One choice. One breath. One sacred yes at a time.

Chapter 13 Bonus Work

Journal Prompts: Embodied Leadership

To prepare for this practice, find a quiet, undisturbed space where you can feel safe being fully present. Remember that this is sacred time with yourself—a reunion, not a performance. You may want to use a journal, speak your responses aloud, or even record them as voice notes. There is no right or wrong way to do this. Let your answers flow spontaneously and honestly, without overthinking. Write or speak freely, allow pauses, feel into your body. After you finish, take a moment to re-read or reflect upon what you shared: you may notice new layers of meaning or emotional truths rising to the surface. Now, ask yourself:

1. What does embodied leadership mean to me?
2. In what areas of my life am I currently leading from alignment? Where am I still performing?
3. What patterns or personas have I outgrown as I step into my truth?
4. When do I feel most rooted in my own authority?

5. What does it feel like in my body when I'm leading from truth instead of fear?

6. What kind of leader am I becoming—and who am I no longer willing to be?

7. How do I hope others feel in my presence? What are the qualities I wish to support, transmit, inspire?

Embodiment Ritual: The Leader Within

This ritual will support you in calling forth and nourishing authentic leadership.

1. Stand tall. Close your eyes.
   Feel your feet planted firmly on the earth.
   Inhale deeply through your nose. Exhale audibly through your mouth, as though saying *"ahh."*

2. Place the palms of both hands over your heart and speak these words aloud: *"I am here. I am ready. I am the one I've been waiting for."*

3. Repeat this three times—each time louder, clearer, and more certain.

4. Open your eyes. If possible, look at your face in a mirror. Hold your own gaze, lovingly, with soft and gentle eyes. Speak your name, then powerfully declare: *"[Your Name], I trust you, and follow you now."*

Let this be your soul's agreement to rise.

Leadership Visioning Practice

This is a sacred conversation with your Higher Self. You can either write it down or speak it aloud, letting your intuitive words flow through you as they come.

To begin, call in your higher self: "Dear Higher Self, please show me the leader I'm becoming. Let me feel her. Let me meet her. What qualities do I embody? What frequency do I radiate? How do I serve? How do I speak? How do I move through the world?"

Allow the response to flow—unfiltered and unedited. You may be surprised by what comes through. Save it. Date it. Revisit it when doubt creeps in.

Energetic Seal: The Real Work Begins Here

You've walked through the curriculum.

You've met the spiral.

You've felt the edges of your becoming.

You've remembered who you are—and who you're not.

Now comes the most sacred part:

Living it.

Not for approval.

Not for performance.

But because your soul says yes.

You are not here to blend in.

You are here to be a living transmission of truth.

To speak what others silence.

To feel what others numb.

To choose alignment—even when it costs you comfort.

This is leadership.

This is embodiment.

This is your medicine.

And we're waiting for it.

We're not here to perform healing.

We're here to live it—so that others remember they can, too.

Epilogue

The Ceremony of Becoming: A Return to Wholeness

If you've made it here, then you've walked with me—
through the pain, the joy, the mess, the clarity, the undoing,
and the becoming.

You've taken the classes no one teaches—the ones where the
lessons are hidden in heartbreak, detours, synchronicities, and
sacred rage.

This was never about graduating from pain.
This was about remembering your wholeness.

We don't get a diploma for awakening.
But we do get a new way of living—more honest, more
embodied, more aligned.

We don't "arrive" on this path.
We return, again and again, to the place we were always
meant to be:
Ourselves.

So, here's to you:
To your sacred syllabus.

To your inner child.
To your wild self.
To your higher self.
To the version of you that chose to come to Earth, knowing
it would be dense, and still saying yes.

May you never again abandon yourself.
May you live your truth unapologetically.
May you walk your path boldly, even when you walk alone.
May you become the version of yourself that your soul
remembers.

And when the next lesson comes, as it always does—
may you meet it with curiosity.
Not because you need fixing.
But because you are a student of the stars.
A keeper of ancient knowing.
A tutor in the classroom of becoming.

You're not behind.
You're not too late.
You're right on time.

This isn't the end.
This is your beginning.

Now go live it.
Fully.

Planet Earth University

Honestly.
Magically.

With love,
Jessica

Closing Invocation:
A Return to Wholeness

Take a breath.

Place your hands on your heart.

Feel your feet on the Earth.

You are here.

You have walked through fire.

You have cried oceans.

You have danced with shadows.

You have remembered your light.

In this moment, you are whole.

Not because you are finished—

but because you are willing.

Willing to show up.

Willing to feel.

Willing to remember.

So, we invoke the presence of your highest self—

the version of you who already knows.

The one who was never lost.

The one who walks beside you in every breath.

We honor the Earth beneath you,

the guides around you,

and the soul within you.

Repeat aloud or in your heart:

"I am no longer who I was.

I am becoming who I was born to be.

I remember.

I return.

I rise."

You are not broken.

You are blooming.

And this is your sacred becoming.

This is your Planet Earth University.

Appendices

Appendix 1: Map of Consciousness

This map, originally developed by Dr. David R. Hawkins, offers a framework for understanding the energetic frequency and emotional tone associated with various states of consciousness. It is not a ranking of worth, but a sacred mirror for reflection, growth, and embodiment. Use it gently. Let it speak to your inner awareness—not your ego.

What you'll find below is a simplified, black-and-white version formatted for this book's print requirements.

For a color-enhanced and expanded version, including in-depth explanations of each level, real-life examples, and additional tools for integration, please refer to Dr. Hawkins' published works listed in the Resources section.

Level	Frequency (Log)	Emotion	Life View
Enlightenment	700–1000	Ineffable	Is
Peace	600	Bliss	Perfect
Joy	540	Serenity	Complete
Love	500	Reverence	Benign
Reason	400	Understanding	Meaningful
Acceptance	350	Forgiveness	Harmonious
Willingness	310	Optimism	Hopeful
Neutrality	250	Trust	Satisfactory
Courage	200	Affirmation	Feasible
Pride	175	Scorn	Demanding
Anger	150	Hate	Antagonistic
Desire	125	Craving	Disappointing
Fear	100	Anxiety	Frightening
Grief	75	Regret	Tragic
Apathy	50	Despair	Hopeless
Guilt	30	Blame	Evil
Shame	20	Humiliation	Miserable

A more detailed exploration of this framework, including full-color charts and deeper insights, can be found in these books by Dr. David R. Hawkins:

Power vs. Force, Transcending the Levels of Consciousness, and *Letting Go: The Pathway of Surrender.*

Appendix 2: Consciousness Shift Log

A Sacred Practice of Emotional Elevation

Use this page as a sacred self-awareness ritual—a space to witness and support your emotional evolution. Complete it as often as you feel called. Let this be your place of reflection, compassion, and conscious transformation.

Date:

_____

Trigger / Moment That Activated Me:
(What happened? What stirred something in you?)

_____

_____

_____

Emotion I Felt:
(Be honest. Name it without shame or explanation.)

_____

_____

Planet Earth University

Where I Felt It in My Body:

_____

_____

Estimated Frequency (From Map of Consciousness):

_____

_____

What I Needed in That Moment:

_____

_____

_____

Emotion or Frequency I Chose to Move Toward:

_____

_____

Practice I Used to Support the Shift:

_____

_____

_____

Insight or Message I Received:

_____

_____

_____

_____

Appendix 3: Spiral Reflection Map

Use this spiral as a tool to visually track your healing journey. Each loop outward can represent a new layer of growth, an emotional season, or a return to an old pattern with deeper awareness. Let this be a space where you witness your own evolution—not as repetition, but as sacred return.

(You may draw a spiral here manually or print one to paste in this space)

Center Point: Origin or Key Event

_____

_____

Loop 1:

Theme or Trigger:

_____

Insight or Lesson:

_____

Phrase or Frequency Claimed:

_____

Loop 2:

Theme or Trigger:

_____

Insight or Lesson:

_____

Phrase or Frequency Claimed:

_____

Loop 3:

Theme or Trigger:

_____

Insight or Lesson:

_____

Phrase or Frequency Claimed:

_____

Loop 4:

Theme or Trigger:

_____

Insight or Lesson:

_____

Phrase or Frequency Claimed:

_____

Loop 5:

Theme or Trigger:

_____

Insight or Lesson:

_____

Phrase or Frequency Claimed:

_____

Loop 6:

Theme or Trigger:

_____

Insight or Lesson:

_____

Phrase or Frequency Claimed:

_____

Resources

Throughout this book, I've referenced various healing modalities, therapeutic systems, and transformational frameworks that have supported me on a path of healing and awakening. The following resources are offered for further exploration—not as doctrine, but as invitations. Let your intuition guide you toward what best serves your own unique unfolding.

Human Design

A system that synthesizes astrology, the I Ching, Kabbalah, chakras, and quantum mechanics to reveal your unique energetic blueprint. Learn how you're designed to make decisions, use your energy, and interact with the world.
Explore: www.jovianarchive.com

Enneagram

A powerful tool for understanding core personality patterns, emotional fixations, and soul-level growth paths. The nine types illuminate both the shadow and potential of our inner motivations.
Explore: www.enneagraminstitute.com

Quantum Healing Hypnosis Technique (QHHT)

Developed by Dolores Cannon, QHHT guides clients into a deep theta state to access past lives and the Higher Self for healing, insight, and transformation.
Learn more: www.qhhtofficial.com

Institute of Interpersonal Hypnotherapy (IIH)

A state-licensed school offering comprehensive training in clinical, transpersonal, and interpersonal hypnotherapy. IIH is where I received my certifications and foundational training.
Explore: www.instituteofhypnotherapy.com

ESCANVI Services — My Private Practice

I offer integrative, trauma-informed sessions for emotional recalibration, energetic alignment, and soul-level healing. My approach blends clinical hypnotherapy, transpersonal methods, energy medicine, and intuitive soul guidance to catalyze deep, lasting transformation.

These sessions are designed for those ready to move beyond coping—and step into embodied sovereignty.

Signature Sessions include:
– Subconscious Reprogramming & Nervous System Reset
– Inner Child Healing & Emotional Integration
– Rebirthing Breathwork
– Past-Life & Ancestral Healing

Book a session or learn more:
www.escanviservices.com/services

The Sovereign Frequency Blog

Ongoing reflections and transmissions on healing, embodiment, personal truth, and conscious evolution. This is where I share what no one taught us—but every soul is remembering.

Read more: www.escanviservices.com/the-sovereign-frequency

Acknowledgments

To my parents —

Thank you for loving me fully and as best as you could.

Your love planted seeds I didn't always understand at the time, but I do now.

And I honor you for it.

To my siblings—the ones by blood and those that life gifted me—

Thank you for walking beside me in this lifetime.

For the laughter, the lessons, the reminders of where I come from,

and who I continue to become.

To my teachers—yes, even the ex-husbands and the full cast of characters—

Thank you for your role in this incarnation.

You were part of the curriculum. You showed me what needed to be healed,

what needed to be released, and what I would no longer carry.

To the guides—seen and unseen—

Thank you for whispering when I stopped listening,

for holding me when I fell to my knees,
and for walking me home again and again.

To the souls I've served through this work—
Thank you for allowing me to witness your remembering.
Your healing deepened my own. You are all part of this page.

To life—
Thank you for every plot twist, portal, heartbreak, and
synchronicity.
You've been the greatest teacher of all.

To the future cast of characters, lined up already—
I await your entrance and your lessons, delivered through
love and expansion.

And to myself—
The one who stayed.
The one who showed up when it would've been easier to run.
I see you now. I love you.
You are free.

About the Author

Jessica Meléndez is a hypnotherapist, energy medicine practitioner, and conscious leadership mentor committed to helping others live in alignment with their truth. Before stepping into transformational work, she spent over two decades in engineering and corporate leadership, guiding multimillion-dollar projects across the construction and infrastructure sectors. As a certified Project Management Professional (PMP®), she brings precision, systems-thinking, and grounded strategy into her holistic practice.

Born and raised in Puerto Rico, Jessica embodies the fierce softness of her roots, the clarity of lived experience, and the fire of a woman who has remembered who she is.

Her private practice blends clinical hypnotherapy, energy medicine, and subconscious reprogramming to support emotional regulation, nervous system balance, and inner leadership. She specializes in helping high-functioning individuals and visionaries release outdated conditioning and reconnect to their power.

Jessica's writing is rooted in lived wisdom and poetic clarity— inviting readers into a more sovereign, authentic, and soul-connected way of being.

When she's not guiding clients or writing, she's exploring ancient lands, soaking in sunsets, or creating systems that bring healing into boardrooms and breath into burned-out spaces.

Let's Stay Connected

If this book moved you, challenged you, or awakened something within you—I'd love to hear from you.

If you're ready to dive deeper into your healing and remembrance, I invite you to explore hypnotherapy, guided journeys, and energy medicine sessions with me.

Visit: www.escanviservices.com
Follow: @escanviservices.jessica

Leave a Review
If this book resonated with you, please consider leaving a review on Amazon. Your words help others find this work—and remind them that they're not alone on their journey.

This isn't goodbye—it's the beginning of a more aligned you. And I'm honored to walk beside you on this most sacred path.

www.ingramcontent.com/pod-product-compliance
Lightning Source LLC
Chambersburg PA
CBHW021636120626
46545CB00002B/564